ROSALIE WILL

SONGLEADING

A WORK OF ART

EDITED BY JOEL EGLASH

TRANSCONTINENTAL
MUSIC PUBLICATIONS
A Division of the American Conference of Cantors

SONGLEADING: A WORK OF ART
By Rosalie Will, edited by Joel Eglash

Copyedited by Debra Corman – Design and compositing by Joel Eglash
Illustrations by Kyle Gorzowski

Transcontinental Music Publications Executive Committee:
  Joel Eglash, Cantor Lauren Phillips Fogelman, and Cantor Steven Weiss
American Conference of Cantors: President, Cantor Claire Franco; COO, Rachel Roth
TMP/JLicense Customer Support: Stacey Berliner – TMP/JLicense Production Assistant: Rose Snitz

TRANSCONTINENTAL MUSIC PUBLICATIONS / JLICENSE
A DIVISION OF THE AMERICAN CONFERENCE OF CANTORS
The world's leading publisher of Jewish music since 1938
1375 Remington Road, Suite M – Schaumburg, IL 60173
847.781.7800 – tmp@accantors.org

Distributed by Hal Leonard Publications
Printed in the United States of America – 10 9 8 7 6 5 4 3 2 1
Item number 994051 – ISBN 978-1-7366908-4-0

TranscontinentalMusic.com
JLicense.com
RosalieWill.com

This book is dedicated
to the memory of

JONAH MACCABEE DRESKIN, *z"l*

who loved life, loved Judaism, and loved music.
He would have been proud
to help raise a new generation of songleaders.

The Jonah Maccabee Foundation
which has underwritten this publication
keeps Jonah's memory strong
by "turning love into action"
through support of the arts, social justice, and Jewish life.

—Cantor Ellen and Rabbi Billy Dreskin
Aiden Dreskin, Katie Dreskin Boonshoft, and Mark Boonshoft
The Jonah Maccabee Foundation (jonahmac.org)

For my children, Tahlia and Arielle.
You bring me joy and are my hope for the future.

For David,
who makes everything in my world better (including this book).

Contents

Preface

Z IONSVILLE, INDIANA, is the site of the significant feel-
ings and sounds of my youth. During many hot and mos-
quito-filled days and nights over many summers in the 1980s and '90s,
Leslie and Lee, Andy, Dawn, Ken, Dan, and Emily created magic. True,
mystical, and wondrous magic.

They were my songleaders at Goldman Union Camp Institute.

Sitting at a long sticky table in a humid dining hall or under cool
shade trees in an outdoor chapel, they brought holy sounds out of the
mouths of campers from all over the midwestern United States. We were
kids who came from modest means or who were more well-off, from
tiny towns where we might be the only Jewish kid or from schools with
lots of Jews and large synagogues. We were staff who came to camp summer after summer because that's the only place we felt we could be our
true selves. We were faculty who often used our vacation weeks to hang
out on a hot, dusty piece of land outside of Indianapolis, with our kids
in tow, just so we could be a part of creating a community where young
people could find their voices, live their identities, and find meaning in
their faith—in a safe, fun, collaborative, and creative environment.

At the root of Goldman Union Camp Institute, a member of the
camps of the Union for Reform Judaism, was singing. We sang at least
three times a day, usually four or five. We sang after every meal. We
sang our prayers. We sang in "friendly competition" when it was raining
and we had to wait out a storm inside. We sang at campfires and as we
walked around camp ushering in the Sabbath. When anyone who went
to Goldman thinks about camp, they think about singing.

I loved every minute of singing at camp. I loved standing at my
table with my bunkmates, ignoring the songbook held out to me (to encourage me to sing the correct words). I wanted to sing loudly, sing harmony, and follow the songleader with my eyes—songleaders who stood
in the middle of the room, not on a raised platform, but on the floor
like me, and led us in fast songs and slow, in silly songs and in songs with

words about loving the stranger, about not being afraid when things got hard, about being peacemakers, and about caring for the earth. They'd run between the benches and tables; they'd come up to me and sing in my face; they'd stand in the middle and guide everyone to them in a single chorus, just by the tilt of their head.

We did not hire professional singers, and we did not have bands or backing tracks. There was no auto tune or even, for that matter, any sound systems to speak of in the days of my youth. But we had the best songleaders in the business. They pulled off their magic with just their bodies, their faces, their voices, and their guitars. That was all it took.

And once I became a songleader in my teens, I never looked back. I songled my way through high school and college, I songled after college and before graduate school, and the root of my calling as a cantor and clergy is as a songleader.

When I graduated college and was asked to teach songleading to high school students, I wasn't sure where to begin. I loved songleading myself and I had some skill as a songleader, but to teach it to others? With the guidance of my first co-songleading teacher, Rabbi Robbie Weiner, I taught my first group of young songleaders. In the years that followed, I continued to ask questions about what it takes to create powerful group-singing moments.

Here, I'll nod with respect to the masters: Debbie Friedman and Pete Seeger (both of blessed memory) could get any room of people to sing. They were not the most perfect musicians or singers, and they were songleading not because they could not make it in another career. They believed in the power of each individual voice as crucial to the collective of the whole. And when they stood, in front of thousands at Carnegie Hall or around a campfire of ten, they led with the truest sense of every person's value, of the voice each person brings into the world—with a desire to see and be seen, to create a world of wholeness and peace, and the deep need to do that work with others. That is the songleader's task. Your task is not necessarily to make recording-worthy music (though one should strive to create beauty with a group every time), but to create meaning-worthy music. Create moments of singing that matter.

> *The songleader's task is not necessarily to make recording-worthy music (though one should strive to create beauty with a group every time), but to create meaning-worthy music and moments of singing that matter.*

To believe in the power of communal singing is to believe that the power of singing together is bigger than just yourself. To train generations of songleaders is to imagine that groups of people from every corner of life—secular and religious, children and wise elders, small groups in a backyard or large sanctuaries or halls—are finding their own power, their strength, their deep sense of love for themselves, each other, and the world by singing together.

It's only in writing this book that I have had cause to reflect on why and how I became a teacher of this holy art of songleading, for songleading is indeed an art. There is beauty in leading people into the deep connections communal singing brings to a group. Being a part of a powerful group-singing experience is akin to witnessing great art or to sharing a musical or a symphony with others. It's collective and powerful and shared. And it takes artistry to songlead. It's a craft that takes practice, experimentation, attention, commitment, and work. Real work. It is an art—and perhaps there is a little science to it as well.

And the outcome is electric. Those of us who have been led into transcendent experiences of group singing can easily recall the power of those moments. We may remember a time when our community experienced great loss, and we brought our voices together in a song of memory or of hope. Singing together gave us the path to be fully in the moment and to allow our true emotions to surface. We closed our eyes or looked at those around us, known and unknown, and felt more connected than we had ever felt before. Our voices rose and fell with the group, held together by the power of each others' voices.

We might remember a life-cycle ceremony; a ritual or a gathering to celebrate new life, new love; a gathering for the struggle and hope for peace and justice. We remember the closeness of bodies together, the vibrant harmonies, the clapping of hands and tapping of feet. It gave us energy and it gave us purpose.

We emerged from those experiences feeling more connected to others, to our own humanity, and to something beyond ourselves. We carry with us all of these moments still because singing together matters. Some would even say it saves lives. In our most vital and defining moments, we are compelled to sing, and we sing together. Whether at a young age at a summer camp or as an adult who finds a song circle, the impact of communal singing is proven to strengthen our health and our hope.

This is why we songleaders do what we do. And like all things that matter, it is worth investing the time to do it well.

My intention with this book is to convey both the values and the value of spending good working time on both the art and the science of songleading. In over three decades as a songleader and in over twenty years as a teacher of songleading, I have gathered the best techniques, learnings, pitfalls, tricks, and tools from leading with and singing with extraordinary songleaders.

There is always more to learn. To this day, whenever I participate in communal singing, my teachers show me new ways of leading song. New ways to help me find tricky notes, or remember a lyric, or bring the right intention to a particular song.

The task of writing this book comes to me in this moment, but I stand on the shoulders of the following inspirational people:

- My first songleaders at Goldman Union Camp
- Those who led the youth services at Shaare Emeth (St. Louis): Emily Bruder and Rabbi Ken Chasen
- My teachers at URJ Kutz Camp: Rabbi Robbie Weiner, Cantor Shira Nafshi, and Cantor Billy Tiep
- Those from whom I learned for so many years at Hava Nashira: Merri Lovinger Arian, Craig Taubman, and Cantor Jeff Klepper
- Those who pushed me to think about songleading in new, challenging ways: Billy Jonas, Joey Weisenberg, and Yara Allan

I continue to walk the path of this work with two partners with and from whom I'm always learning, practicing, coaching, reflecting, failing, and getting up to try it all again: Cantor Ellen Dreskin and Dan Nichols. The lessons in this book belong to them as much as anyone—and now I give those lessons to you to help guide your songleading journey.

Acknowledgments

THERE ARE MORE SONGLEADERS in my life than any other people. My decades at camps and as a cantor have brought me close to the best in the business. And my work as a teacher of songleading has brought me close to the talent, dedication, and joy that so many young people have toward a desire to create meaningful communal singing.

There are many that I can and must thank by name. Cantor Ellen Dreskin, Cantor Jeff Klepper, Dan Nichols, Merri Lovinger Arian, and Rabbi Dan Freelander read early drafts of the book and kept me honest and on point, offering invaluable feedback, love, and support. Alan Goodis, Rabbi Leora Kaye, and Rabbi Ken Chasen have been treasured friends and confidants and always challenge me (and my assumptions) in the best ways, which allows me to continue growing. The Hava Nashira faculty over the past few decades are an integral part of this book— from you I learned countless lessons by watching, debating, struggling, dreaming with, and making music with you. You are artists and teachers who have the deepest integrity and know what it means to lift up others through singing.

The participants of Hava Nashira, Shabbat Shira, the URJ Teen Songleading Fellowship, the Songleading Major at Kutz Camp, and the leaders and participants of Songleader Boot Camp all are woven into the stories and experiences I share here. My songleading has been made better by those with whom I sang and those with whom I have taught.

Joe Eglash has been a friend and colleague for a long time. From our time together at the Union for Reform Judaism through our work with the American Conference of Cantors, Joe has always put his love of Jewish music and the art of song at the forefront of his work and his life, and I have loved working in parallel (and often in tandem) with him over these many decades. As the director of Transcontinental Music Publications, he and his team at TMP and at the ACC have done a remarkable job lifting up the value of the diversity of Jewish music to celebrate communities of every background.

Joe's confidence in me and this project was endless, and the opportunity to put into writing something that is in my bones was a joy and a privilege, and sometimes a daunting task.

Joe and I together are deeply grateful to the Dreskin family and the Jonah Maccabee Foundation for so generously providing the funding that made this book possible. We are honored to help carry Jonah's legacy. We thank the TMP executive committee—Cantor Claire Franco (president of the ACC), Cantor Lauren Phillips Fogelman, and Cantor Steven Weiss (ACC TMP chair)—and the staff and leadership of Transcontinental Music Publications and the American Conference of Cantors past and present, including Rachel Roth, Stacey Berliner, and Rose Snitz. The excellent illustrations that help make clear the ideas in this book were created in partnership with artist Kyle Gorzowski.

David Billotti, the best writer I know, helped me organize my decades worth of experience into a usable book and helped take what were sometimes vague theoretical techniques and word-painted them into meaningful sentences and paragraphs. He also never let me give up or feel too overwhelmed by the task. He ever and always believes in me.

And for all those songleaders who are just starting to lean into this sacred work: thank you. Songleading is not easy work, but it is the most rewarding work I know. There is great beauty in creating moments that change people's lives. There is an art to bringing individuals together from diverse experiences and beliefs and who walk different paths of life, then building a single uplifted vocal sound. If you are committed to building singing communities, to helping people feel less alone in the world, to guiding them to deepen their relationships with others and with their world, to enhancing their sense of the Divine and to their deepest selves, then there is so much to be hopeful about.

I can't wait to be led in song by your spirit, your joy, and your love.

Cantor Rosalie Will
Pesach 5782

Introduction

SINGING TOGETHER MATTERS. Group singing is the glue that holds many communities, particularly "opt-in communities" (such as religious organizations, summer camps, youth groups, justice organizing events) together or at least creates a sense of shared purpose and shared accomplishment that influences the desired vision of the group's existence.

Most cultures use communal singing to create a sense of egalitarianism—that even if there is a "leader," our differences among social strata or jobs become insignificant in the sharing of song together. No one person stands out (in solo), nor does one group get preferential "musical" treatment because of their status. It can be one of the great equalizers in our world, if handled thoughtfully, with intention and in collaboration with everyone involved in the creation of the experience.

Any strategy for becoming a successful leader of communal singing must start with why. Why do we sing together? Why do we need leaders to sing together? What is our role as songleaders in facilitated communal singing? I will come to this point again and again in the following pages; it is the foundation for anything you might do as a songleader.

In my experience, when a songleader says to a group I'm a part of, "This is my favorite song!" or "You're going to love this piece!" I find myself wary. Our job as songleaders isn't necessarily to share what we want to sing, but rather to create the opportunity for the members of the group with whom we're singing to be moved, to be transformed, or to learn something about themselves or the world.

To be sure, a songleader has to care about the content, derive pleasure from sharing it, and believe in its value. But the energy and commitment to any piece of music comes through the experience of singing it together, not because a songleader told the group how much they love the song.

I believe that for a songleader to connect most deeply with a congregation, audience, or group, they must first be willing to connect deeply with themselves. It is only by clarifying your purpose and intention that you will be able to bring your most authentic self to the work.

Here are a few questions for self-reflection before we begin:

- Why does singing with people matter?
- What moves me about singing with other people?
- What do I hope to receive from leading song with others?
- What or how do I want a group to feel when we finish singing together?
- How can I use my gifts and skills to create meaningful singing moments and to be of service?

Once you've built this solid foundation of introspection, then you are ready to move on to the "how." That's what I hope to show you with this book.

If you are a real beginner to songleading, it might be easy to become overwhelmed with so many choices and techniques. Here are a few ideas and tips to just get started:

- Attend a songleading workshop and ask to lead one song for feedback.

- Ask your community if you could lead one song at an event.

- Young students as well as elder communities are always looking for music and song and can be very forgiving and wonderful places to do your own "learning by doing." Volunteer to lead a song with children in a school or with an elder community as a way to begin to refine your craft.

WHILE PEOPLE ENTER THE WORK OF SONGLEAD-ING from many directions, I lay out the technical work here as linearly as I know how. There will, of course, be overlapping ideas, as each piece is part of a whole, and one decision, however slight, will influence another choice or outcome.

You could look at the chapter headings and focus on one area in which you'd like to improve or look to one piece of the songleading work that seems interesting or helpful. Be prepared that it may hint at principles or techniques referenced in other places in the book and that you may find yourself exploring other areas. You also can read the book from start to finish. I move from general theory and preparation to actually leading music with people, then to how the work might need to shift and grow if you work with others or want to continue to deepen your own development.

You may have noticed that the chapter on repertoire is at the end of the book. (Aren't songs the first thing a leader of songs needs?) Of course, you will find references to how song selection impacts your work throughout the book. However, the order of the chapters is purposeful; I believe that sequence to be the best service to those you are leading. There's a lot of work to do before you finally pick the repertoire.

Many of the chapters will conclude with a summary, a bulleted list of points, or a checklist of items to remember or questions to ask. There may be references to appendixes. In addition, knowing that songleading in different locations invites different techniques, I will often differentiate between a worship setting, a school setting, and a communal setting. Numerous chapters may cover a very general songleading principle or technique, but when appropriate I will offer specific strategies in those three areas as a way to assist in your work in particular environments.

I define a **worship setting** as a prayer or spiritual gathering where certain constraints or rules may apply regarding a text or creed or certain spatial limitations exist around an altar or ritual focal point. Sometimes a worship setting may actually be a ritual of some kind—a joyous event, installation, dedication of a space, or life-cycle event. The worship term for these sections includes prayer services with liturgy as well as rituals for sacred gathering.

School settings are for those who lead music in schools, not formal music in a public school, but a place where we invite young people to sing together (such as a religious school or a sing-along in a youth or teen space).

Communal settings are a bit of a catchall, but in my experience they are for singing before a social justice rally or march, a breakfast or luncheon for a community civic event, or an interfaith gathering or celebration.

Another note on terminology: in most instances, I refer to those you are leading as the "group." For our purposes, "listeners" is too passive, "audience" is too performative, and "congregation" is too specific.

Joe, Kyle, and I spent a lot of time discussing how to create illustrations that were inclusive and celebrated the idea that anybody can be an effective and inspirational songleader if their instrument (be it voice or guitar) is tuned and their heart is in the right place. Inclusivity is a core value of both my professional and personal life. If we didn't get it right, we apologize—but perhaps you can help us by doing your work no matter where you're from, what you look like, or how you got here.

You might be wondering, who is this book for? If you are new to songleading, you can use this book as a foundation from which you can build your own unique identity and style. If you are a more experienced songleader—maybe even more than me—you can use this book as a refresh of the fundamentals or as a guide for teaching your own students.

I suspect, though, that many of you are somewhere in between. It is my hope that the alchemy of a new idea or a reminder found in these pages mixed with your own experience and a little stage fright leads to experiences for you and those you serve that are meaningful and memorable. However you use this book, I hope it also reminds you to find, as Jewish tradition teaches, the intersection between the *keva* (the proscribed routine) and the *kavanah* (our intention in the moment). That's where we create our own magic.

·1·
Know Your People

OVER THE YEARS I'VE LEARNED that in addition to techniques I can use in the moment, the more I know ahead of time, the better suited I am to create successful singing with people with whom I do not have long-standing relationships.

I frequently travel as a musician/clergy-in-resident and arrive at a congregation's Friday night Sabbath worship knowing only a few members of the clergy or lay leaders and no one else. While my preference would be to have come a day earlier or have spent time with members of the congregation in advance of worship, that is not always possible. This creates a challenge for me, in that part of my role with the congregation is to invite the community to lean into new ways of thinking about prayer or of music and movement as a part of a spiritual practice. But if the people don't know me, they likely don't trust me enough to be open to the vulnerability of rich singing.

I often spend the first moments of the prayer experience to warm wary faces, who clearly would sing for their long-established clergy and leaders but who aren't willing to take a lot of risk with a stranger.

This is where the questions offered in the introduction come into play. You are on a precipice when you begin your work, implicitly asking people to leap with you into something both known and unknown, predictable and unexpected. You must know why you are doing this and for whom you are doing it in a particular moment. It is your foundation and it is from where the confidence exudes that draws people into the experience you want to create. I cannot say it enough: your primary motivation cannot be to share your favorite song or simply just show off your skills—though of course, our human egos crave affirmation about both of those things. By knowing the why and the who, you circumvent the ego and get to the good stuff.

Yes, we can't completely know the intentions or the heart of every person we sing with! But by not scrimping on the prep work, there are things we can uncover that will help lead us more clearly into the programmatic choices and the repertoire that will build a successful singing experience.

Let's start big and then get specific.

Part of the songleading experience is about building trust among the group being asked to make music together, and that can't happen if you don't have at least a sense of who the people are that make up that group.

Before you try to understand some very specific place and time elements, you may want to know:

- How much emotional capital do they share with each other? In other words, have trust and familiarity been built over time? Will they be willing to be vulnerable with each other and take a little risk?
- What brought them to this moment, and what do they think is going to happen while they're there?
- What is your relationship to the group? Do you know each other and for how long? Will you need to take time building trust, or can you jump right in?
- What can you reasonably expect that they'd like to feel at the end of your time with them?
- What does success look like for you and for the organizers who have invited you to lead?

Most of these questions also apply and are equally important if you are working repetitively or permanently with a community as a leader of song. Knowing who the group is, why they gather, and what you and your partners hope will happen is imperative before every gathering.

Very few people are prepared to break into song at any minute, even if asked nicely by the leader. If a group knows each other well—a class from a school, a team of employees who spend a lot of time together, a day or overnight camp, for example—perhaps they will have already developed the trust among each other to take the vulnerable step of singing together. But many people do not like to sing in their homes in front of their own family, let alone sing in front of strangers or acquaintances.

Knowing what the educational goals of a group are will help you understand what kinds of content the group should be singing together.

Our instinct may be to start with "What should we sing? Here are some songs I love." Of course, you must have some commitment or connection to the repertoire and truly believe it's the right content, but that's not the place to start.

Here are some examples to help you think this through.

Perhaps a leader has asked you to lead singing for their group, and you plan to teach and engage them deeply, only to learn they just wanted background live music that people can jump and dance to and talk over. You may be able to convince the leadership that the group should be given the opportunity to do more, but then you should be aware of how the environment may work against that.

For example, you may be on a large outdoor stage, with booming sound, and the group of participants is much smaller than the large space they have to stand in (there are no seats), and so they roam and talk and are positioned very low and far from you. The loud sounds only drive the participants to talk or scream over the sound, and therefore you are simply in the background. You would have wanted to know in advance where you will be standing in relation to the participants, whether you have sound support, and if everyone has access to lyrics.

Taking the time to know your group beforehand, to truly understand what has moved them previously and what they might be expecting from you, will help you to build trust quickly.

In addition to space considerations, you will need to know where the group has been before you will be singing with them and where they go after. Are the kids heading to a dance? Their delightful singing will be unsuccessful if they're dressed in fancy clothes and full of nighttime teen energy in anticipation of a dark dance, when you had hoped to have them make sweet harmony in concentric circles.

Without passing judgment on any of these kinds of experiences, part of our potential success lies in our ability to know when we are only able to provide what's being asked of us. This does not mean that we don't try to engage in a meaningful way, but we now have clarity about what the leadership wanted for this moment.

Perhaps the answer "FUN! Just a rockin' good time!" will help you manage your expectations. Or the answer "Some content on this particular theme, and some good singing, and winding down moments" may lead you to ask more pointed questions about the space or setup you have tentatively been given, which can then be adapted to help everyone (you, the participants, the leaders) feel like it was a worthwhile experience and the leadership's goals have been met. Knowing your group means more than knowing the people in your group. It means understanding what's being asked of you so that you can be prepared to respond appropriately.

Let's consider each of the three settings mentioned in the introduction.

Worship Setting

While leading worship is a specified skill (and can be discussed in other writings or coachings), some of the strategies and tools we would apply in any leading of song can help guide our worship leading in specific ways as well.

The question of who gathers for worship is a complex one. Whether in a church, synagogue, or meeting hall for a spiritual or prayer experience, people come for different reasons. A community of regular returnees still each have different needs and different life experiences. All the more so if you're working with communities who are trying to open doorways for people to find safety, comfort, and communion with others but who will not know the rituals, traditions, and well-known melodies of a given group. If you are a visiting worship leader, and not a leader with long-standing relationships with a community, what are you to do?

Consider:

- What does it mean to pray in this community?
- Is there an area of liturgy or prayer in general that the leadership would like the community to be focused on?
- What are the "sacred cows," the elements of your worship that are crucial to create safety, familiarity, and trust among the congregation?
- Will you have the opportunity to be in relationship with the community before you lead them in prayer?
- What does the space look like, and is there any flexibility?
- What would you like the participants to say they have experienced as they leave your time together?
- In conversations with professional and lay leaders, ask about the makeup of the community and who they expect to attend the

worship. Has there been a loss to recognize or a joyous event to celebrate?

- Where are you in the life cycle of the community, the calendar of their religious tradition? Where are you in the life cycle of that institution or community—for example, the installation of new leadership or dedication of a building or new student group?
- Do people travel great distances to join in fellowship, or is it a local/walking community? Do people come with families? Are there usually children (and if so, of what ages), and what is the expectation about decorum/noise/youth involvement?
- What is the vision and mission of the congregation, and how is that manifest in the worship and musical choices of the community? Does the community lean into social justice and use prayer as a way to galvanize the commitment to sacred work in the world? Or do they value moments of silence, introspection, solitude, and meditation?
- Will the people know each other and value relationship building within the worship, or is the goal more to be moved and led by leaders "at the front"?

School Setting

One of the lessons I'm constantly learning and relearning is about the "before and after" of singing with a group—understanding where the group has been and where they're going. Is the classroom just returning, grudgingly, from recess, most likely highly energized and not interested in sitting still and learning? Or are they going to recess after we sing, therefore somewhat distracted and restless, needing their physical activity? In both cases, I would prepare to lead a song with physical movement and gestures. This "up on your feet" song could, in the former circumstance, open the singing session as they return from recess. In the latter, it could end the set as a way to lead them into physical activity or perhaps be placed mid-set if they are too excited to go outside and get restless. Keep in mind that it may be very difficult to settle energy for more relaxed singing after participating in a physical song.

Whether you are the guest of a community once or in an ongoing support role, you will want to know where the group is in their year, educationally or pedagogically, with regard to preparing a presentation or a celebration, a holiday, or a milestone in the community. Knowing who the group is in their communal setting is crucial to selecting repertoire and style of singing.

Here are examples of questions you could ask before singing with children or youth:

- Will there be other staff support in the program with me? What is their expectation about their role (are they on an "off-hour" coffee break, or do they help me as leading partners and in engaging with students)?
- Where will the children be coming from as they begin singing time and where are they going to when my session is finished?
- Is there any educational content, learning, holiday, or value that the teachers are currently working on that I could reinforce or use music to enhance?

Communal Setting

Most communal justice gatherings have some kind of musical content. The first instinct by organizers is often to invite a musical performance of some kind, and all too often the idea of a communal singing moment is either an afterthought or not given much attention—and it's often the first to get cut to save time. And yet it can create the necessary moment of cohesion, spirit, or energy to move a group forward. Encouraging moments of real communal singing when gathering for justice is a worthwhile endeavor.

In most social justice gatherings, knowing who will gather is crucial. There are usually complex political, communal, and perhaps even religious sensitivities even as we gather to support a similar cause. Understanding the goals of the advocacy or justice will involve learning whether this group is just being formed, with the hope that they become longtime allies to foster longer-term relationships for community organizing, or whether they are a returning group of allies with a history of gathering together.

Knowing the timing for the group is also important. You may want people to get up on their feet if they've been sitting a long time and are, for example, preparing to head out to the street after you sing. Conversely, your singing moment may precede a testimonial of someone affected by the issue at hand. This will impact the energy you establish.

Your physical proximity to the group as well as their placement in space is something you want to know in advance. For example, whether the group is outside in the heat or sitting inside at round tables impacts how and what you sing. This information can almost always be gathered in advance. We'll look at space considerations more closely in chapter 2.

Life-cycle rituals, building dedications, or celebrations of a milestone also will attract a very specific group of people. Understanding the ages, communal contexts, previous experiences, and familiarity with the moment at hand will help you prepare.

Here are some questions to ask:

- Are groups from different communities, clubs, or faiths gathering, or is it a fairly homogeneous group?
- Who are the other presenters, speakers, or musicians who might be sharing content? Is there a chance to partner with them and learn more about what they will be offering?
- What do the people gathering expect to happen? Why are they there?
- Who is the point person who can help you make changes on site?

The more you know about who is in the group you will sing with, the better you can prepare repertoire and determine the style in which you songlead. Whether it's a small family gathering for a life-cycle event or diverse cultural groups coming together for a large community social justice action, knowing who people are, what they come with, and what you hope they leave with leads to meaningful, resonant singing.

☙

Taking the time to know your group beforehand and to really understand what has moved them previously and what they might be expecting from you will help you to build trust quickly, get connected faster, and deliver an experience that is tailored to the group in front of you.

For a concise list of questions to ask about your group, please see appendix D, "Know Your People," page 118. For more information on establishing clear goals, see appendix F, "Setting Goals," page 122.

Know Your Space

ONE OF THE GREATEST OBSTACLES TO SUCCESS-FUL SINGING—and sometimes the most difficult to change—is the setup of a room. But you can create success in most spaces if you have prepared for what the space can offer and what it can't and have considered beforehand other tools you can employ to create meaningful singing.

Collecting information from those responsible for managing the space (whether it's one you use regularly or you're coming in as a guest) is important. The first question to ask is, where would you be standing and do you have any flexibility of movement? Are you raised above the group (on a dais, podium, or worship platform) or on the same level with them—and do you have the option to change that?

There are a few reasons that the position of your body in relation to the group is important. The most important, of course, are sight lines. The group needs to see you and you need to see the group, but don't stop there. You might think you can see the group just fine when you are standing on the floor and they're standing in front of you, but it may turn out that you can only see the faces of the first few rows. The group should be able to see your face and as much of your upper body as possible. Critically, you should be able to find every face and make eye contact as much as possible with each person. Remember, part of your job is to make connections. So, lines of sight between you and the individuals in the group (not just the group as a single entity) is important.

If it's possible, I encourage you to familiarize yourself with the space beforehand if it's not known well to you. Perhaps you can suggest other options of rooms or locations that better fit the goals as you understand them for your singing. If you are aware of the number of participants expected, choose a room that will fit them snugly. It's often better for group singing to have more voices in a small space rather than too few voices in a large space. Try to provide options for you and the folks you are asked to sing for by deciding together what space will be most successful.

Let's begin with being raised up in a higher position than the participants. How high above the group will you be? If you are in a long or very large room, you might want to be elevated so more people can see you and so you can see how the group is connecting. Perhaps the sound or the acoustics are not so good and you will need to rely more on your body, height, or your guitar, if you use one, to communicate visually with the group. If the group is standing, it may also be preferable to be raised one level above them—perhaps on a podium or a step. *[See figure 1.]*

If they are seated theater style or even at round tables, you may want to consider being on the floor with the participants, knowing that you still have some height if you are standing and they are seated. If the group is seated on the floor, a platform will create too much elevation, so standing on the floor may be better but still too high above, and you may choose to sit on a stool or a chair in front of the group. But this may limit your ability to be mobile as you sing. I have found that a stool is sometimes a good choice rather than sitting the way the participants are, especially compared to standing over them. A stool can be a nice compromise; it allows you to stand when you need to but also to slightly lower your body when that feels important as well.

When considering all of these possibilities, remember that your primary motivation and what the group expects of you will probably differ (and needs clear intention) for every experience. This will help inform your decision.

For example, if the work you have been asked to do involves creating more intimate moments among the group, perhaps being on a raised dais with little mobility will not allow you to get close enough to your group. You then have a few choices. You can ask if you can move to the floor to be level with the participants. Or if you must be on the platform for some reason, work with the team to refocus what success looks like and what kind of singing will be successful in such a space. If intimacy cannot be expected given space limitations, perhaps another kind of connecting musical moment might achieve parallel goals. You could, for instance, use an accessible call-and-response tune where the group can feel ownership and you can feel close to the group.

In some spaces the participants will be lined up in seated rows.

NOTICING YOUR POSITION IN RELATIONSHIP TO THE GROUP IS IMPORTANT.

IF PEOPLE ARE SEATED AND YOU'RE ON A HIGH PODIUM,
YOU MIGHT BE TOO FAR FOR INTIMACY.

NICE AND PROXIMATE BUT WITH SOME CONTROL –
GROUP ON THE FLOOR, YOU ON A CHAIR.

IF PEOPLE ARE SITTING ON CHAIRS, GET A BIT HIGHER BY STANDING.

IF PEOPLE WILL BE STANDING,
YOU WILL PROBABLY NEED SOME HEIGHT TO BE SEEN.

Figure 1

You might have intended to create opportunities for movement—if not around a room, even in each person's personal space—but you find that the pews or chairs are fixed to the floor. It is helpful to know this before you plan for people to bend over or spin around; when a group is limited in its ability to do what you ask, they become frustrated and confused, and it's hard to maintain a relationship. If the chairs can't move and the participants must sit there, you would adjust your repertoire accordingly in advance.

Sometimes we are asked to sing in a large room with a small group and the participants are scattered around, far apart from one another, taking up a lot of floor space. *[See figure 2.]* Should we sing from the floor at the front? From a raised podium? What about the participants? Where should they be? Do I have the ability to guide their movement? Will I have a team of partners to help? We might want to call everyone to come closer—some will do so out of a sense of being helpful and dutiful; many will not. More might come forward, but then drift back into the empty spaces over the course of your singing time. That is a natural result. If possible, you could see if the venue has trees or plants (or something similar) to control the back of the space. *[See figure 3.]* Either way, trying to bring them closer signals that you are considering their experience and trying to connect.

One tool worth trying is to use the corner. There are two ways to do this. You could stand in the corner, with the walls coming out on either side and the people fanning out (either standing or sitting on chairs), looking into the corner toward you. This has a way of focusing people's attention, physically and optically: the walls become the arrows toward you, so you might gain some control over some nice singing. *[See figure 4.]* One pitfall is that sometimes people toward the back of the group will still start backing up into the larger part of the room, talking and creating distance. It is human nature to find space and fill it. Consider bordering off the area with the same trees mentioned above.

Another option is to reverse that setup, depending on the size of the group and how much time this might take. Arrange the participant space starting with the corner and moving out, while you stand closer to the center of the room and face them. *[See figure 5.]* This is something that is better planned ahead, if you know the room is not conducive to good, close singing.

Often, surprises emerge once you arrive in a space. You might need

THE ROOM IS TOO LARGE FOR THE NUMBER OF PEOPLE;
FOLKS SPREAD OUT.

Figure 2

BRING THE FEW STANDING FOLKS CLOSE
BY CLOSING OFF THE BACK OF A SPACE.

Figure 3

**PUT YOURSELF IN THE CORNER SO THERE'S FOCUS,
AND CLOSE OFF THE BACK TO MAKE A SPACE SMALLER**

Figure 4

PUT THE PEOPLE IN THE CORNER FACING THE MIDDLE,
WITH YOU FACING THE INTO THE CORNER

Figure 5

to troubleshoot in the moment. Do you want everyone to get closer to you and to each other? You could ask everyone to grab a chair and create a semicircle of chairs in front of you. Or is creating one big circle an option or a good idea? Even with advanced knowledge of a space and a well-developed plan based on an understanding of your environment, you could find that in the moment it has significantly changed. This is where your ability to stay calm but still see what you can change to better meet the needs of the group and find ways to be successful will become crucial.

Perhaps a quick physical rearranging of the setup will fix the problem. A songleader should always be prepared to do the heavy lifting of moving chairs, asking other folks to help as needed. Allow extra time once you arrive to set up the room exactly as you will want it; consequently you will not feel frustrated later about the lack of success of the room when you might have been able to change it to your advantage.

> *It's helpful to have a few ideas of how to move—yourself or the people—to ensure that you can achieve the goals that you and your group have set out and to maximize singing opportunities.*

As someone who has worked both front-of-house and back-of-house for events of all sizes, I want to mention here that quite often the person (or team) setting up the space is a volunteer, is inundated with other responsibilities, or is part of a labor union with rules belonging to the facility. There may be very specific reasons that you are not aware of for why a space is set up the way it is. We want to make the situation the best it can be so you can meet the goals agreed upon with the group. Also, be both flexible enough and prepared enough to be able to adjust as needed as you move along. Your singing moment is important, but remember to consider the larger context and the humans who also have obligations in the moment.

And, unfortunately, sometimes the space is the space, and for whatever reason, making changes is impossible. You are unable to move any chairs or to reorient yourself in relation to the group. Your choice in this case is either to stick to your plan and hope it works or have other songs, ideas, and engagement options ready to use if the space gets in the way of your original singing goals. We'll address this later, in chapter 9.

SONGLEADING OUTDOORS

I am often asked to sing outside, particularly with young people. It's seen as a great way to get folks out of the confines of a school or classroom and, I believe, to align the freedom of being outside with the fun of singing. Who doesn't love to be outdoors (weather permitting)?!

Being in nature, seeing the world around you, is a wonderful way to express ourselves. I love to sing songs about the earth, creation, and the environment while out of doors.

Yet there are a few important challenges to consider, and share with your leadership, before you commit to singing outdoors:

- Sound does not reverberate as it does indoors. It disappears into the wide-open space. If you want to hear beautiful singing from the group, as well as your own, that is hard to achieve outdoors.
- Sound amplification will be crucial for the above reason. And when the wind blows it will make distracting noises into your microphone.
- Unless you're in a very controlled location outside, it's easy for people to sit far apart, roam, and therefore create distance. Consider how you can "block" people into a close area near you.
- Things like grass, bugs, hot sun, and dirt can be distractions.
- Will people be expected to sit on the grass? Is someone bringing out chairs and intending to return them? Does the terrain and seating arrangement work for people who might have physical challenges, or do respectful accommodations need to be made?
- If the weather becomes inclement, where is the alternate location?
- If there is some unexpected disruption from outside the group or space, what is the contingency plan?
- If you need materials like lyrics for yourself, where will they be? If you plan to use a music stand, bring clothesline or binder clips to attach your pages to the stand, or they will blow away.
- If the group needs lyrics, will they get paper handouts, assuming there is no outdoor projection screen? If you have screens outdoors, consider the time of day and the ability to see the screens in broad daylight.
- If it's very sunny, you might find it more comfortable to wear sunglasses. I strongly encourage you not to. While it's uncomfortable to squint, I believe that wearing sunglasses while you songlead

cuts off the community and makes it nearly impossible for the group to sing along, particularly in an already challenging environment.

We all will be asked to sing outdoors, and we should do so when appropriate to the event and audience. The goal is to be prepared for what you can reasonably achieve with less than ideal acoustics, many distractions, and challenges to yourself and your group.

> For more information on songleading outdoors, please see appendix G, "Songleading Outdoors," page 123.

SINGING IN THE ROUND

Before we get into particular settings and how space might be approached differently in each one, I want to devote some extra attention to singing in the round and lay out some general principles and concerns. Many of us believe singing in the round is a preferred way to sing. Circles have always been a shape that indicates egalitarianism. When you picture people in an intimate meeting, a recovery group, a team who leaves the office to become more relational, or a cabin or camp setting, it feels collegial and communal. It can be very meaningful to see each other's faces—to feel the sense, within a circle, that there is no beginning or end, no distance or hard edges to the space, and no one person separate from another.

Singing in the round is also a powerful way to hear sound coming from others. When most of the group faces front, you hear the person singing behind you (maybe) and the people on either side, but the leader is the one who receives all the sound, not the participants themselves. Singing in a circle allows people to look around to one another and to gain confidence from seeing others move their mouths. The exposed physicality and vulnerability that comes with singing in the round often produces the best kind of sound, because it requires everyone to lean into it, let go of some inhibition, and together create something shared and powerful.

Many challenges arise with singing in the round, though. For one, the physical placement of the leader is always in question:

• Should you stand in the middle? If you do, your back will be to

**YOU STAND IN THE MIDDLE OF A LARGE SINGLE CIRCLE OF CHAIRS.
YOU MAY HAVE YOUR BACK TO FOLKS AND MAY NEED TO SPIN AROUND.**

Figure 6

some of the participants all of the time. Not only will they not be able to see you or your mouth and body cues, but they will not be able to hear you at all. You could turn around to reach everyone as you're singing, but again, at any point half the group will not hear or see you *[See figure 6.]* Your goal of a circle may be to create cohesion and unity, but if you are facing one or two people, the people to whom you've turned your back will feel the opposite. They will feel left out or unsure of what to do.

- If you sit as one of the members of the circle and it is a large circle, then folks across the way may not be able to hear or see you. You benefit from a sense of equal participation, but depending on the size of the group, you may be farther away from a few people than you would if they were all in front of you. *[See figure 7.]*

- Another option with you as a member of the circle is to create multiple circles, one inside the other. In this way you can get more proximate (perhaps there are 8 people in the inner circle, 12–15 in the next one, and then 20+ further out). While you may be closer to some people, you will still have your back to some. You also have the issue of there being numerous circles, instead of one cohesive circle. *[See figure 8.]*

When thinking about singing in the round, you must consider any complementary visual content (such as screens or other participants or leaders) and where it will be in relation to the circle. What about sound, microphones, or acoustics? Is there a partner sharing the leading with you? Are the people familiar to each other, or have they never met? Any of these could impact the success of circle singing and the vulnerability and risk at play.

Finally, a crucial piece to consider is accessibility—both for those who may need easy egress or have a mobility aid like a wheelchair or cane, as well as what those at the "back" of the circle experience. In any circle (a single circle or multiple concentric circles), leaders often put the chairs right up against one another to create as close of an experience as they can around a large circle and to invite the intimacy they're trying to create. And yet, if someone is "inside" the circle and needs to leave, they will find themselves climbing over the space between the chairs. They might become a distraction, which may cause the participant anxiety and guilt. If the person has a mobility aid or needs to move quickly to

SIT INSIDE THE LARGE CIRCLE,
CLOSE TO SOME, FAR FROM OTHERS.

Figure 7

**POSITION YOURSELF INSIDE OF THE TIGHT CIRCLES,
WHERE EVERYONE IS VERY CLOSE.**

Figure 8

**WHILE YOU ARE INSIDE MULTIPLE CIRCLES,
THERE IS STILL AN ACCESSIBLE ENTRANCE FOR PARTICIPANTS.**

Figure 9

attend to an emergency of any sort, they could become panicked.

Many people with accessibility needs (such as those with physical or emotional needs, caregivers, people with children, or emergency hospital personnel) spend their entire time in these experiences, designed for connection or uplift from communal singing, worrying about how they might egress the circle easily should they need to. Creating an inclusive and accessible environment is a core value of what it means to create a sacred singing space. *[See figure 9.]*

If you have multiple concentric circles and some are invited to sit close but others are not sure they want to be so close to the action, do you inadvertently create an "inner" and "outer" circle of engagement? Perhaps you may intend to do that, but if someone arrives late and does not want to climb across rows of chairs or navigate with their mobility aid through a tight formation, they are relegated to an outer circle and might feel far from the experience.

These questions are rooted in the same principles we've discussed up to this point: the "why" of any singing gathering and the willingness to be of service to the group. What do we hope to accomplish, and who are the people who will be with us?

Let's look at how our choices about space are impacted by setting.

Worship Setting

The spaces in which we worship are complex and vary between and among faith traditions and denominations. Some worshiping communities move locations regularly, and others have a very fixed sanctuary where all prayer happens. The questions about space usage are often limited by inflexible, preexisting architecture like a raised platform, fixed pews, mandatory podiums with microphones, and more. But even within limitations, there are questions such as these that you can ask and decisions you can make that will impact success:

- When might it be helpful to be on that raised platform and when might you want to stand on the floor closer to the participants? Will you have a sound system that is portable in both locations? Will people in the back be able to see and hear you clearly?
- Are people looking down into text, a book, or a handout? Do you need to get their attention to indicate any musical moments with your body, instrument, or facial cues? Are people looking at screens above you, behind you, or next to you? Where is the best

place to stand? Should the focus be on the screen or you, or are there opportunities for both?

• Is the worship music designed to create communal singing, or are there moments for reflection and meditation? What space usage might help you achieve each of those styles of engagement?

• Are there partner participants such as co-clergy or other leaders, and where are they located? Is there a choir or a band, and are they the focus? Is the congregational voice the focus? Where are people's eyes drawn, and are you aware of and in control of that choice?

In some worship spaces you may have the flexibility to design your own space, with movable seating or a reorientation of the room. Perhaps you would like the seats laid out in a horseshoe or U-shape so that you can be front and center but allow people near the sides of the room to curve inward, see across toward one another, and create a more enclosed sound.

Remember, the questions about other elements still apply (screens, sound equipment, other presenters, etc.). Consider whether you want people seated in more than one row—closer to you and each other but two or three people deep—or if you want everyone in a single row. You will need to know in advance how many people you expect and what you'd like to achieve.

Some community organizers suggest having fewer chairs than you need and adding chairs as the audience builds. This helps to ensure that people don't take the farthest-away seat and that the group is not so diffuse. In addition, singing is usually better when more voices fill smaller spaces. The sound fills more robustly and the group feels the power of its own voice. You might also consider intentionally choosing a room that is more snug.

Singing in the round can be effective in many worship situations as well. Many are encouraged to sing their prayer when they hear and see others singing and making eye contact with each other, communicating shared purpose. On the other hand, some people find the vulnerability of knowing that someone is watching you sing or engage in music or text that is unfamiliar to be daunting and off-putting, and it discourages participation. Unless the group knows they are coming primarily to sing (as opposed to mourn a loss, celebrate a milestone, or sit in solitude and intimacy with God), it can be stressful to be forced into a small circle. It's particularly important in this setting to consider how well the group knows each other and what your goals are. Sometimes strangers might connect through singing in the round, and others find it too frightening.

You can change the space by changing your proximity to the group even in the midst of the worship, without moving any furniture, but instead moving yourself! Perhaps if much of the prayer is led from behind a lectern or podium, you could step out from behind it and move toward the group. Or choose a moment that might be helpful to come off of a raised platform to get close to others, and then at the right moment return to the platform. Consider how this works in the context of the song, possibly using this movement to add drama or intimacy at just the right moment.

School Setting

When working as a traveling songleader, you may be asked to visit classrooms or different communities where people are already seated when you arrive. This again is where you should ask in advance (or visit to observe, if at all possible) what the setup is so you can be prepared.

Will the students be at round tables? Some may have their back to you and grumble when asked to turn around. Will they all be seated on the ground but you have no chair to sit on (or a very tiny student's chair) and must stand, thereby creating distance from your group? Are you placed in front of a window where the students will be distracted by other kids on a playground? The information will affect the choices you make.

Singing in the round can be very effective with children, particularly if the group is not very large. If you are able to sit on the floor with the children (and not all leaders are, so as administrators we should not insist that our leaders all sit on the floor when they may not be able to), you can create the proximity to height and sight by looking at everyone. Seeing everyone's body, hands, feet, and faces can be helpful when singing together.

Perhaps your music requires that kids be able to move around. Are you asking them to move a lot but they are seated at chair/desk combinations or round tables that are very close together? Will the children have full freedom of movement in their space? Will they be in a large space where they can easily move farther away from you and your control? Will you need to be able to have access to each student, to get close, to tap someone, or to pass out an object?

All of these questions are crucial to help you in two areas. First, you may decide to request a change in setup in advance or upon your arrival. You may need the staff (whom you will have ensured will be there in advance) to help move a room around quickly. Second, if the space cannot be changed, then you need to plan your content to meet the space you are given. You cannot sing a song with full-body movement if all the children are stuck at desks, but if they will be able to move their arms, choose repertoire that makes those moments successful.

Questions about the size of a room, where students are or can be positioned, and what your physical proximity is to them has a huge impact on your success and can affect the repertoire you select if you know the space constraints or opportunities in advance.

Communal Setting

Communal environments are often the least flexible in terms of adjusting the space. More often than not, because the singing is one small portion of the program, sometimes planned at the last minute and therefore not the main focus, you will have the least influence and impact on setup.

This is why, for singing in a community gathering, board meeting, or social breakfast, you should be prepared with lots of repertoire and ideas in your back pocket. (Again, this is covered in chapter 9.) You may plan the perfect piece for the purpose of the gathering—a group of women celebrating the changing of leadership of their chapter or a group of teens preparing for a march—and find that the physical setup will render that choice impossible. Perhaps the group gathered late and will need to leave early because the local police had to alter the planned path, or maybe the room is much too big for the number of people who showed up.

This is where your skills as an observer of what's happening in front of you, of what the current group in the present situation needs from you, must take precedence over all the practice and thinking and dreaming you did about the perfect singing moment. Space can both elevate and disturb successful singing and it's important to keep focused on what was asked of you, what's reasonable to expect, and what's achievable in the moment in which you find yourself.

Here are some issues for which you can prepare:

- Some people may sit (if there is limited seating or seating provided for those who are unable to stand for long periods) and others are standing.
- The room is much too big for the number of people gathered.
- The attendees are excited and ready to go, and you experience lots of talking and a lack of focus.
- Placards, signs, and banners are causing sight-line disruption.
- There is mediocre or no sound support.
- There are changes to timing—less or more time for singing—with little advance notice.

ℭ

We most often find ourselves in anything but the ideal scenario, no matter how much we plan and prepare. We all will find ourselves in rooms that are challenging for singing, and it's helpful to have a few ideas of how to move either yourself or the participants to give yourself the best shot at making a strong connection. You have many options that can help you make the best of the situation. I urge you to bring with you an open flexibility and generosity of spirit. That is usually enough to ensure that you will be well received.

> For more information on spatial considerations, please see appendix E, "Know Your Space," page 120.

·3·
Know Your Body

SONGLEADING IS A HEAD TO TOE EXPERIENCE. From the top of our head to the soles of our feet, each part of our body can be used to communicate effectively to a group. Indeed, beyond the notes, our job as songleaders is to create energy, feeling, connectivity, and power. Our bodies help the group as much as our voices or our words, not only for accuracy in the actual song, but in atmosphere and experience. Our bodies are as equal a part of successful songleading as is our voice or our instrumental accompaniment. So we must use our bodies intentionally and also effectively.

Now, of course, no two bodies are alike, and we all access the built world differently. The opportunity to use different parts of our bodies as tools for songleading does not mean that each tool is crucial to be successful. Our bodies meet the world in myriad ways and are designed uniquely. You are you, and the more you bring your own gifts, the stronger your people will respond. The best practice is not to have a "Standard Set of Songleader Movements." We are not landing planes; we are bringing our full authentic selves to the moment, with the hope that our people will respond in kind.

In the spirit of "why," being told by a songleader how to sing sometimes feels demanding, and it can make people wonder what your intention is. But, when you demonstrate with your body that the song is growing in intensity and feeling, it is contagious. Mirror neurons click on and the participant responds accordingly.

FEET/KNEES/LEGS

Starting at the bottom, with our rootedness, how we use our legs, knees, and feet will help dictate how the group learns to follow our lead. Just like groups follow the leader by walking in their footsteps, our feet and knees can indeed help us "lead," even if our group remains seated.

The first thing to consider is where you're standing. As we learned when we considered space, where you place yourselves in a classroom will make a huge difference as to how you're able to communicate with your group. The same applies outside the classroom.

If the group is in rows or a concert-style mass in front of you, you have to decide how much you move around while you lead. If you choose to move, ask yourself, "Where am I going, and what am I going to do there? Where do I need to go next?" Don't wait until you get to a place and then wonder what you're doing there. Do not just pace around because moving indicates "active songleading." It can also suggest nervousness or lack of intention.

Conversely, should you plant yourself firmly and stay primarily in one place? When thinking about the goals you want to achieve, will standing still allow for a more commanding performance that may be needed in the moment?

Either work, but there are pros and cons of both to consider:

Wandering (moving around, back and forth)

Pros: This is a great way to access folks who are far from the song-leaders. If you are intentional about where you're going, you might get close to one section of folks in order to regather attention or invite them to sing more with you. In this example, you should move toward them, stop, make direct eye contact and indicate what you'd like from that section, and spend a little time there; then move back to where you started or intentionally toward another group who needs your attention.

Cons: As a default strategy to show "engagement," wandering is not useful. It can cause distractions as people struggle to follow the moving songleader in space with no direction. The group will not be able to stay focused on your face, your voice, and your body if they have to constantly maneuver to see you while you wander.

Planting

Pros: If you have been moving around in order to engage groups who are on the fringes, there may be times when you want a specific focus on you, and you stop suddenly and stand still. This might draw focus for a new unfamiliar part you'd like to teach or signal that a deep, expansive, or meaningful part of a song or moment is arriving. A confident and clear centering can help make that possible. You should not move unless you have somewhere to go with intention. A strong planting can create clarity of focus.

Cons: If you stand still for a long period of time, you may lose the interest of people on the sides or at the back, or the group may tire of looking at one spot for so long. You also might find you have less flexibility in your body to create cues or visual hints to the group. It will keep the group rigid and not relaxed, free, and joyful.

Our feet can also be used as accompaniment. You can stomp as an indication of rhythm or tempo. Lift your leg in preparation to stomp slightly ahead of the beat to make sure you can accent a certain moment or come down on a certain beat together. If everyone is headed toward a big entrance all together, you can lift your foot high enough to be noticed (and well in advance), so that in a slightly exaggerated manner you can stomp or plant your foot down in an obvious way so in that moment everyone enters together.

The knees are also a very useful part of our lower body. *[See figure 10.]* If we are teaching and know that a tricky melodic phrase will drop many tones or that a phrase starts much lower than where the previous line ended, our knees can be our best friends. When you drop your body low in anticipation of that, the group knows instinctively to go down. They do not have to be musicians, or read music, or even sing in key. The physical visual cue tells them what sound to make.

I've watched groups I'm leading drop their own chin a bit and lower their eyebrows themselves when I cue to go down low by dropping my chin and lowering my eyebrow; they then reflexively sing a lower note (and it's usually the one I wanted!). Their own physical reaction to yours helps their sense of where we should be in the music.

The same is true in the opposite direction, with the tiptoes. *[See figure 10.]* If you can exaggerate going up on your toes (and match the move with your head and eyebrows, to be discussed shortly), this will also indicate a move upward. If the second part of a line or part two of a song starts a bit higher, before we come in together at that entrance I will have gone up on my tiptoes to show that the higher part will happen next. Many folks will use the neck of their guitar to indicate a lifting in pitch, but without guitar or even with one, tiptoes can help. It also creates contrast against the lowering of the knees for other moments.

YOUR LOWER BODY HAS LOTS OF PERFECT SONGLEADING TOOLS.

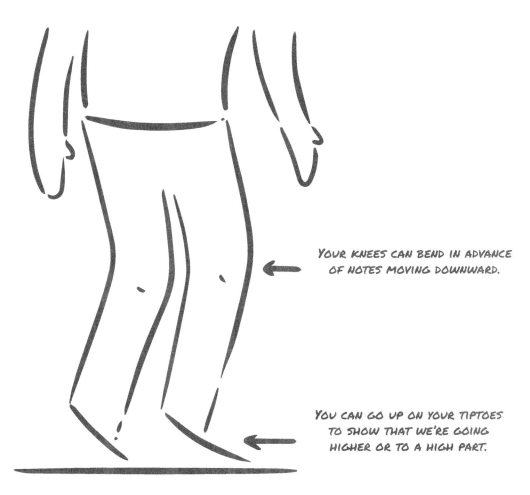

YOUR KNEES CAN BEND IN ADVANCE
OF NOTES MOVING DOWNWARD.

YOU CAN GO UP ON YOUR TIPTOES
TO SHOW THAT WE'RE GOING
HIGHER OR TO A HIGH PART.

Figure 10

ARMS/TORSO/SHOULDERS

Our body's middle section is a great place for a lot of songleading direction as well, although I don't find it quite as effective as the feet/knees or the face/head.

Whether or not we have a guitar in hand, our arms are extremely helpful not only to communicate a change in pitch but also to invite a group to feel a certain way or to lean into certain moments. Stretching arms wide or throwing a single arm up in the air tells a group to just let go—to sing big and broad and open. It's more effective (and less intimidating) for a group to sing with more robust energy when the leader throws up an arm than they would for a leader who yells, "Sing louder!" or "More!" The arms can also help people know when to hold a long note and just soar, and enjoy the power of the group sound. *[See figure 11.]*

Our arms and hands are also very effective for communicating the movement of pitches upward or downward when we are teaching or reviewing a newer melody. Places of transition in a song may require our hands and arms to help the group remember what change is coming. The key to success with all body techniques is to practice them, both by yourself in front of a mirror and with others as well, to get feedback about what's effective and what is not.

"Pitch leading" is what we call using our hands or fingers to help the group know when a tone is moving up or down. When practicing pitch leading with a finger, hand, or arm, you must also prepare very carefully. You will be more successful if you practice before you decide to use your hands to help a group with pitch. It can be confusing for a group when your hand goes up when the pitch really goes down!

A good tool is to identify for yourself where "home" is (in musical language, the tonic or the root) on your body—in other words, the note where most phrases may start or end and the place at which the song probably starts or ends; the comfortable home. If "home" is always at about chin level, then you should always be at your chin for those notes. If we start part B of a song on the same note as "home" that the majority of the song begins and ends on but your hand is down near your stomach, folks will get confused.

If you want to remind the group that a note repeats (groups want to be helpful by moving all around and therefore are usually surprised when notes repeat), you could poke your fingers forward in the exact

YOUR ARMS ARE GREAT SONGLEADING TOOLS FOR CUEING THE GROUP.

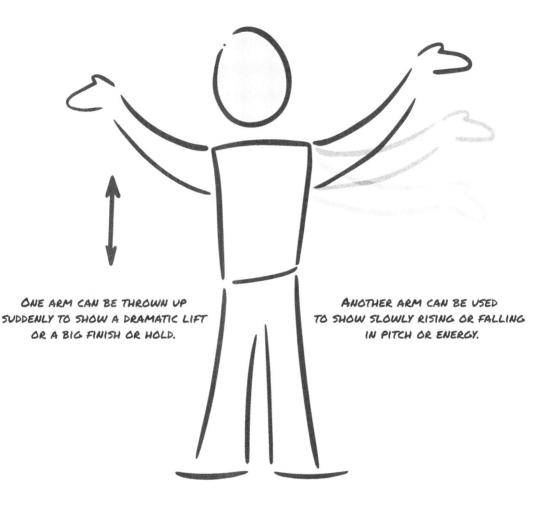

ONE ARM CAN BE THROWN UP
SUDDENLY TO SHOW A DRAMATIC LIFT
OR A BIG FINISH OR HOLD.

ANOTHER ARM CAN BE USED
TO SHOW SLOWLY RISING OR FALLING
IN PITCH OR ENERGY.

Figure 11

same place repetitively. If your hand moves around, the group will too. Or if, for example, the third line starts high, your hand has to be thrown up significantly higher than where you have been hanging out around "home." And as you lead the song, if you continue to use that gesture at those specific moments, the group will find it easier to remember those subtle or tricky changes over time.

Of course, too much can be too much. Resist the temptation to indicate every note of the piece with your hand. If there are one or two tricky passages with a few unexpected notes, I find it most effective to slacken the pace and move my hand slowly. I'll usually do this only when we are moving around a lot of different tones, for instance, or to sing a line in the song that starts in an odd place. I'll also use my fingers to remind a group that we stay on the same note for the next part. I'll drag my hand across my body, like an arrow across the plane of my body on a horizontal trajectory, to show the group that we should keep singing the same note, or I'll hold the note out loud for a while to connect it to the next, even if a breath should come there. It's a way to create a connection between those same notes.

A more advanced technique is to use two hands, with fingers facing each other, and put the other hand in an exact line with the first hand to show that the next note is in the same place as the first note. If I've noticed that the group always wants to jump up there and I need to remind them to stay still, I will use my other hand to show that the next phrase is on the same note we are ending on.

Our shoulders are very useful parts of the songleading tool kit. If the move you'd like the group to make is smaller than what a deep knee bend or big arm movement would require, the shoulders are helpful to convey to the group a tiny upcoming shift. My esteemed colleague Merri Lovinger Arian calls it a "shoulder-note," a melodic movement that is a subtle half-step or a slightly off-sounding change. The slight shoulder movement helps the group lift ever so subtly. *[See figure 12.]*

The way to achieve success in much of this body work, particularly hands and arms for pitch direction, is to make your move just before the moment arrives. If your hands or fingers are moving perfectly in time with the song, it is of no help to the group, even if it looks good or seems to be correct in terms of placement of notes in "space." To be of service to a group, moving your hands a bit ahead of the notes that you and the group are singing in time will give them a chance to move

IN ADDITION TO YOUR FACE AND ARMS, YOUR SHOULDERS ARE HELPFUL –
LIFT ONE TO SHOW A SLIGHT RISE OR LOWERING OF A SINGLE NOTE.

MERRI LOVINGER ARIAN CALLS THIS A "SHOULDER NOTE"!

Figure 12

in the right direction before it happens, so that the landing happens in time.

> *The intent of working hard on technical cueing considerations is not so that the piece of music sounds perfect when sung by the group; it's so that the group feels the power of their own voices, experiences the success that comes from connecting with one another through making music, sings about values and ideas that matter, and harmonizes or creates new sounds with just what they have with them.*

NECK/FACE/BREATH

We have reached the top!

If you are seated or are leading singing online, your neck and face are particularly useful. But even in a large room, with perhaps more exaggerated moves, our neck, head, and face are the most important parts of our songleading body. Our head and neck are useful to indicate to a group when to come in.

As I've explained previously, you would need to lift your head and drop it on the beat on which you want folks to sing. This means that you need to lift your head, in anticipation, before that new strong downbeat so that your exaggerated chin drop or strong head indication of a beat occurs at the exact same moment as that beat. If you wait until the strong downbeat to lift your head in preparation to bring it down, it's too late. The moment is over.

It's most helpful to nod on the beat, at the moment you want them to sing, as long as they've seen a slow, slightly exaggerated lifting of the head to know to prepare to join you on the downbeat. Imagine your head as a conductor's baton, going up in the air as an invitation to cue the orchestra that we are about to begin. You can also crane your neck to cue the group that the next part, line, or half a line will start a bit higher, or go higher. It simply helps let the group know what to anticipate musically while you teach new repertoire.

If you are leading a call-and-response song and you want the group to respond without verbally telling them it's their turn, you can lift your head as you finish your call phrase and nod with your head, as it were, at the group to come in for the response. Or if you are teaching something new and you want the group to repeat after you, you need not always say, "Now you!" Sing your part while holding still and then nod as you finish, and the group will know it's their turn.

Your face is a key tool in accomplishing your work. In addition to the chin as it relates to our head nods, your face (including eyes and eyebrows) can provide assistance too, and as with the previous body movements, they tell the group what to anticipate.

Using our eyes and especially eyebrows to indicate upward motion or even that the group should focus on you for a cue that may be coming (a sort of "watch me, something's coming" moment) is helpful to build a successful songleading style. If you are sharing something new, or less familiar and your voice, the guitar chords, and strum tempo are all working together but your face is perfectly still, the group will not clearly know or remember the different parts of the song. They may become discouraged if they don't hear themselves sound like they are singing the tune decently.

I am told that I have excellent use of my eyebrows, but this is only due to employing them in my songleading for so long. If the group is not too large, I can lift my eyebrows before a moment where the pitch will go up, and folks will follow. Sometimes I raise one eyebrow and lean to the side, and the group understands that it's a tiny melodic half step or a crooked kind of lift. The result is that I'm getting the response that I want—and the listeners are feeling connected and like they're singing well—without me having to verbally instruct or cajole them.

Finally, we have our breath. It is the thing that keeps the flow not only of our singing, but of our sense of connection to everything and everyone. While of course we imagine that everyone is breathing while they sing, you can use your breath in multiple ways:

- Allow time for a dramatic inhalation to help the group know when to breathe or that a long phrase is coming up.
- Take a big breath to cue the group that we are about to start a piece, versus just starting singing and everyone having to play catch-up.
- Breathe to set intention for the singing session or gathering. We root ourselves in the space as well as to a common group breath. Perhaps create a breathing rhythm that's in line with a moment or song the group will sing.

You could even talk about the breath. If you have to rush to take a breath or have time for one, use it as a teaching moment.

I led a morning worship song once that had a long phrase followed by a long break in the notes before the next phrase began. I noticed that people wanted to jump in early, before the break was over. So, I used a few of these full-body techniques: I started by dragging the neck of my guitar slowly across to show we weren't ending. I also sang the note a bit longer than the group—I had snuck a breath in to get ready—so the group wouldn't feel the need to fill the empty sound too early with the next phrase. When those strategies didn't always work or I wanted more from the experience, I changed tactics. The song happened to fall around a morning ritual of acknowledging our body and breath, re-claiming our spirit as we started our day. So in that empty space in the song, I said something like "We have time here to enjoy our breathing, to really remember that it's there, and that it's a gift that will keep on giving." Or I could have said, "Don't worry about the next line, your breath will guide you to it; you'll know. Like starting our day with breath, don't rush it."

Using space and breath, I helped the group feel something differ-ently about the piece while also teaching them about the value of taking a breath.

The lengthy focus on all of these technical cueing considerations is not so that the piece of music sounds perfect when sung by the group, nor is it a way to make sure we have a lockstep choral group.

Instead, it's so that the group feels the power of their own voices, the success that comes from connecting with one another through mak-ing music, singing about values and ideas that matter, harmonizing, or creating new sounds with just what they have with them that day. This is the dynamic and life-changing power of group singing. But without our awareness of what the group needs and our directed and thoughtful full-body guidance, they are less likely to feel that.

As always, it is important that you both prepare for the moment beforehand as well as being present in it when you are actually there and adjust accordingly. The moments during which you lead with repertoire that is familiar to the group, you will of course need to provide less di-rection. Your job is to set the tempo and key, and then they're off. You could indicate to watch you for a slight ritard when you're coming to an end with a head nod and an eyebrow lift, or instead of shouting, "Last time!" lift the headstock of your guitar to the group so that they know to watch and are aware that something is different (you are coming to a close).

But for any songs that are new, newer, or not yet part of the entire group's canon of easier songs, our job as songleaders is to help the group to succeed, to help them know what sounds come next (remember that they are relying solely on you—their own musical memory cannot be a guarantee), and to help them enjoy moving through newer repertoire, because the reward is so great.

Before we're done with the body, let's consider this in the context of the settings.

Worship Setting

Teaching new material in worship is more complicated, as we'll discuss in more detail in chapter 5.

But for review, or even for familiar liturgy that has multiple parts, some body indications can still be helpful. Yet in a sacred space, more careful sensitivity to the room and participants is required, as well as sharper clarity and awareness of the goal.

If one of your worship goals and values is successful singing, you will need to understand whether you are singing repertoire that the group has become familiar with over time or whether it is new to them and then design your leading to be inclusive and geared toward helping everyone feel connected to the prayer music. You will likely use your full body to help a group move into various parts of a piece of liturgy or any of the communal singing around liturgical moments, but in a different way. In fact, you may use your body a bit more than your voice for instruction. For example:

- Rise up slightly on your toes to indicate the second part (which is higher than the first).
- As you finish a verse that is designed more for a meditative-listening prayer moment, you gently lift your head, nod, lean forward, and smile at the group, indicating you'd like to hear *their* voices for the chorus.
- Raise an arm inviting the group to sing more deeply and fully at that moment in the worship where you sing your hopeful yearning for peace, for the commitment to work together once you leave the sacred space, and when you sense the power of the moment and want all voices to build.

School Setting

Most teachers—especially teachers of young children—will tell you that to keep their wandering attention, everything must be just a little bit more animated. In this space, you might find greater success if you exaggerate the movements a bit.

If you're seated in classrooms to be closer in proximity and height to children, you will really need to use your head, neck, and feet on the ground more to indicate what should happen.

Communal Setting

Depending on the location, community singing might require that you use more vocabulary and verbal cues, but full-body cues are important as well.

In a large hall or ballroom where you may be singing before a rally or before a breakfast to honor an award recipient, there may be mediocre or no sound support. Assuming the group has eyes on you, your body can be especially useful to cue a group.

ℭ

Songleading is a full-body exercise. Being comfortable with your body and aware of how it can complement your delivery will increase the likelihood that your group will sing in a way that is both strong and meaningful.

Know Your Instrument

L ET'S START with where everyone expects a songleader would start: the guitar. Some would say revolutions have been started with the guitar, from Woody Guthrie writing on his instrument, "This machine kills fascists," to Odetta releasing a record of Bob Dylan covers a couple of years after they sang together at the Civil Rights March in Washington, DC, in 1963. Conversely, a guitar in the wrong hands can clear out a room at a party in just a few moments.

You may not need a guitar to songlead, but if you're going to use it, be more like Guthrie and less like that guy.

I encourage you to consider the guitar as a rhythm instrument, which makes sense because most songleaders would not want to sit behind a drum kit! In group singing, the guitar's purpose is to anchor the key (with chords) and rhythm (with strumming and tempo) for the group to stay together.

Here are some tips for guitar usage in songleading:

- The guitar is just a tool; your voice is the priority and should always be louder and clearer on top of it.
- Chords can be used sparingly when needed, as they are a guide for pitch and rhythm. In a pinch, playing just the downbeat chords in key places (to anchor the song) with a single strum will get you far.
- Much of the guitar's purpose is as an extension of the body. You can cue a group that an upcoming note or phrase begins higher on the register or lower. You can articulate that a note will be held straight by pushing the neck (fretboard) of your guitar horizontally. Your guitar can cue to a group that an ending is coming (as they can't know that your voice might slow down or stop). Look for a little more about this later in the chapter.
- Learn and become confident in a variety of strumming patterns, otherwise all pieces will sound the same. Different patterns will

also help a group know how to sing. When you move from part A to part B, if there is a different sound you want from the group's singing, the guitar's job is to help cue the group to what sounds different and how you want the group sound to feel. Just like an arranged song on the radio will have a different "sound" for different parts, the guitar can help you define the mood as you move between parts of songs or from one song to the next, by the variety of the rhythms and usages of your guitar.

As always, keep it simple, and remember that the guitar is not the primary focus. It is too easy for the guitar to become a crutch both physically and vocally.

While utilizing different voicings (chord shapes) and more beautiful chord pattern or solo lines can enhance singing in certain situations, a common trap songleaders fall into (particularly those who come to it from a love of guitar and not necessarily of singing) is to spend a lot of time fine tuning guitar accompaniment only to discover that the guitar is louder than the voice. The group will never really engage vocally or as robustly as might be desired because they aren't sure (or can't hear) where they're being led. The guitar may overpower the group singing and pull the group's focus.

> *One of the common misnomers about the guitar in songleading is that it is equal to the voice in terms of usage and importance. The guitar in context of songleading is a rhythm instrument. In creating group singing, the guitar's purpose is to anchor key (with chords and pitch) and rhythm to help the group stay together and to enhance the musical presentation.*

This does not mean that one can't become more sophisticated on the guitar. For many songleaders, as they improve, the guitar becomes an even more useful tool to create mood and to impact the nature of the singing. But, for someone committed to group songleading, the focus on improving guitar playing beyond knowing your chords and strumming should only come after you have become an expert at leading a song with your voice and using your body to communicate.

Finally, the goal is to not to have to look at your fingers while you're playing, except perhaps for a particularly challenging chord. By and large, if the guitar is a support instrument, you should keep your eyes and face pointed toward the group with whom you're singing, and not bent toward the neck of your guitar, hoping you place your fingers in the right place. Beginners will need to do this, but sometimes making a choice to not play your instrument instead of struggling to move your fingers to different chords is a better choice. The group will become distracted by your focus on your hands and be less likely to sing along.

STRUMMING PATTERNS

The way you strum or pick the strings of the guitar not only will affect the "mood" (read: tempo, speed, and feel) of a piece, but will assist or detract from the group's ability to sing it or have the piece move the group forward in the way in which you are hoping.

Sometimes the 1-2-3 (oom-pa-pa) waltz structure of your strum makes the piece move too fast because there's no space in between those three beats. Similarly, single strumming, one strum per beat, also means that your song may be too fast. But double strumming (two strums per beat) can be tiring for you as the songleader and sometimes create intensity around a piece that may not be the goal.

When selecting a strum pattern for a given communal singing piece, I find that thinking about the physical feeling in the body that I'd like to evoke or where words should be accented is a helpful place to start. Certain on-the-beat patterns create a downward, into the ground feeling (like a stomp or a march feel), while others create a sense of lift, of rising up, or of a bounce, like being propelled forward (indicated usually by more off-the-beat strums).

Some pieces of music need only a single full strum to set the key, perhaps for an open, spacious singing moment. If something has a lot of syncopation and a lot of words, a more interesting pattern will help create the energy (but beware of overplaying and muddying the complicated lyric or syncopation). When holding a long note, at the end of a line or a section or song, resist the temptation to keep strumming and playing. The sound of a group holding a note has power, so let it ring out sometimes—a single strum ringing with the sound of voices can be very powerful. Allow the unity of the group to coalesce around the sound of your guitar.

Often, the strength with which you strum (with a heavy pick or if you're heavy handed) will drown out your voice or the voice of the group. Experiment with strumming with the back of a fingernail or with a medium-weight pick and playing with a lighter touch. Practice with your guitar and voice in a mirror. Play like your instinct is to play, and record yourself—then play it back with a discerning ear. Don't listen and say, "I heard myself just fine," because you know the song so well. Instead, consider: Am I straining a bit to hear the ends of those lines that go low and actually could hardly hear that last word, because the guitar was too loud? Could I play more lightly at those low notes where my voice isn't quite as strong and loud, or should I stop playing and just keep singing so they are clearer?

Beware of playing the low E string when E is not in the chord. This applies mostly to an F chord (if you are not playing a barre chord), A minor, D major, and D minor. Sometimes in our enthusiasm we strum all six strings all the time. That can limit our ability to find nuance in our guitar and rhythm (nuance in different parts of the song or in a full program—all songs cannot and should not feel and sound the same from our guitar). Additionally, it sounds dissonant. Mostly, chords in keys like E, G, A, and C utilize the low E string (if you are playing fairly simple and straightforward chords). It takes practice to come into those strums hitting the fifth string (A) or even fourth string (D) as your root note.

Check your guitar tab charts and they'll tell you which strings not to play. Particularly if you have a heavy strum and a less confident voice, those dissonant low strings can get in the way of creating space for the group to effectively sing nicely with you.

SETTING A TEMPO

I can't count the number of times I've begun a piece with too fast a tempo, usually by playing the guitar intro faster than I wanted to sing. I often start a song with guitar strumming that is too fast because I am nervous and excited (these natural songleading emotions often lead to things being too fast). Sometimes I forget to anticipate where we are going, as I am only thinking about how to begin.

When I feel nervous and exposed, I tend to push the tempo a bit, to appear peppy, engaging, and fun. Then I lose the focus and the desired outcome when I come to the meaty section of the piece.

Now, when this happens and I start a piece and realize very quickly that we are going too fast, I am not afraid to slow down. I am not worried about being embarrassed. I'd rather sing successfully and slow down if I can than just have a runaway train. And, a quick self-deprecating comment will often win the group over.

I have found some strategies for keeping myself from starting too quickly. Here are two options for setting a good tempo in advance (they work best if you are songleading with a guitar but can also be of use if you are not):

1. Begin leading the group with the faster of the two sections, often the "B" part of the song, the chorus, or the place where the song "lifts." In this way, if you set the tempo for the fastest part from the get-go, you are less likely to start the more relaxed (or more expansive, fewer words, lower energy) "A" part too fast and get stuck in that busy B part so fast that you can't keep up with yourself!

    If possible, sometimes beginning the song with that upbeat B part—either at full tempo or even slower, which then gives you the opportunity to build—will help you keep control over the tempo as you go and not leave you stuck on a runaway train.

2. Before you begin, take a moment to stop and set focus, and hum through that B part internally. Feel the strum in your wrist, as if you are playing guitar to yourself, in order to set how fast you know you realistically can get for that B part, without it getting away from you.

    Then, start at the beginning (the A part) in the tempo that will best prepare you to hit the more active B part at a reasonable tempo for yourself and the group. It may feel like you're starting too slowly, but trust yourself; you are preparing to ensure that the more upbeat part does not feel too fast.

Another way to look at this is to consider which part of a song is most important to you, in terms of the mood or feeling that you want to create. Which part matters most in the worship or singing session you're leading and will get the group to feel something meaningful, but also help you achieve the goals you've set for yourself beforehand?

I want to hear in my head *exactly* what I want the group to sound like in the chorus before I start the piece with the first verse. I have to feel the B part (chorus) even as I sing the A part (verse).

The runaway train feeling might occur less when leading without a guitar. This offers another lesson and strategy about keeping your tempo in check: start without the guitar or with minimal guitar.

As I've said before, you should be leading with your voice (and the voice in your head!) anyway. You may need to strum the first chord of a tune to anchor the key. Then, sing the piece without the guitar, singing in the tempo you think is best for the group. As the tune moves along, you could then add a few strums, or strum a single chord as the chords change. In this way, the tempo is more likely to remain under your control. You can add strumming patterns to establish rhythm later.

This serves two useful purposes. The first is that you won't let your guitar playing lead the way. Many beginning songleaders let their guitar lead because they love to play or are just learning and it feels great to practice that guitar. However, newer guitarists may not know as many different strum patterns or have confidence in using the guitar as a song-leading guide, and not as the lead instrument. Without real practice, the tempo of your strumming will set off how fast you sing and often is simply too fast.

Another benefit of starting with less or no guitar (a cappella) is that it forces you to lead with your voice. The long guitar intro or the guitar being the first or loudest element will be avoided if you strum a simple chord to anchor *your* key and then just sing the song the way you want the group to sing it. The vulnerability and fear are a reality, but the openness of your voice and the clarity of tempo and arrangement will help make your piece more successful and help you feel more in control of where you want to take the group in that moment.

GUITAR AS AN EXTENSION OF YOUR BODY

If you lead with a guitar, its long neck can become a wonderful additional tool. As in every other strategy, the key is to know when to use it and to plan its use to anticipate the need within the group, not at the moment the group needs it.

The neck can be used to cue the group about pitch. If the neck of your guitar sits at at about 10 on a clock (if you are the clock, and right-handed), then you can lift it to 11 or almost 12 to signal that we will be going higher (lifting up on your toes, as previously discussed, also helps). If the pitches go down, swing the neck down to 7 or 8 o'clock. *[See figure 13.]*

With practice, you can use smaller motions to use the neck of the guitar to guide pitches up and down for a few in a row. If you go up two tones and then suddenly drop one, you could lift and accentuate the neck movement once, then again a bit higher and then drop it low, all a

THE HEADSTOCK (NECK) OF YOUR GUITAR CAN BE USED
TO SIGNAL THE GROUP TO GO HIGHER OR LOWER IN PITCH.

Figure 13

bit before the beat of the notes you'd like the group to move on.

The neck is also very useful when you are songleading with a partner (more on that in chapter 8). When a good partner turns to look at you for a transition moment, you can use the neck of the guitar (not your voice—they could be far away and you shouldn't shout to them over the group singing) to cue that you are ending or simply to signal them to just watch and listen and that you are making a change. If part B is higher, you could put the neck in the air (here's another chance to use your eyebrows too), and your partner will know you are heading to part B.

Of course, sometimes we miss cues ("I thought you meant part A and you meant part B!"). That's okay too. We are living in the joyfully unpredictable world of communal singing.

OTHER INSTRUMENTS

Of course, great songleading can also be done with piano, accordion, just a tambourine, or virtually any other chording or rhythm instrument. Using a particular instrument requires it own technique, not only in the facility and playing of the instrument, but in how you use it to lead. Piano is a good example of an instrument that, even if you play it well, takes different strategies for songleading. You will probably need to be well versed in your material in order to not look at your hands or your pages, but to look at your group. Some songleaders will lead while standing at a piano, but if you need to sit, I would encourage you to lead to the left or right and not over the top, where it will be harder to see you. Learn to play melody or simple chords with one hand so that you can point out notes and use your body to show the group what to do with the other hand. *[See figure 14.]* Of course, you will want to play chords and melody and make the instrument sound like lovely accompaniment to the singing once the material is well known, but practice playing with one hand and communicating with the other.

If you use percussion (like shaker or tambourine) as accompaniment, be sure to consider when you will want to sing or teach without them and when the best moments are to add them in.

YOUR VOICE AS AN INSTRUMENT

As a songleader focused on singing, you use your voice as an instrument to guide the group toward what you hope they'll sing. You

SUCCESSFUL LEADING FROM THE PIANO JUST MEANS
PLAYING ONE-HANDED SOMETIMES
AND USING YOUR OTHER HAND AND ARM TO CUE THE GROUP.

Figure 14

don't need to play guitar to be a great songleader. Bobby McFerrin is an extraordinary songleader, and he doesn't play guitar.

Whether teaching a new song or just helping the group along, your vocal cues are a key part of communication. "Callouts" are what we use to tell the group what to do. In worship, you probably won't "call out" instructions, but your voice can help guide the group.

Your instinct will be to speak instructions, as we would in a class or announcing a page number. Sometimes spoken cues like "back to the beginning," "let's do that again," or "youth voices only" are very helpful. Find some phrases that are both clear and show your personality.

Concerning inclusion and sensitivity, much has evolved as we think about gender or even gender and vocal ability. Where in decades past we might divide a group as "boys and girls" (assuming boys sang lower than girls), we now can have fun with language like "high voices and low voices" or "left side of the room and right side of the room," so that people can self-identify into which group they'd like to sing. No one will feel excluded.

> *Where in decades past we might divide a group as "boys and girls," we can now have fun with language like "high and low voices" or "left and right side of the room," so that people can self-identify. No one will feel excluded.*

"Sung cues" can be incredibly effective as well. If you are in part A of a song but would like to move into the next section, it can be helpful to "sing" even a short bit of the upcoming phrase that you'd like the group to sing next. Remember, it's unlikely, particularly with a newer piece, that the group will remember how a B or second part begins. Even in a well-known song, if you repeated the first part a few times and you'd like to move to the second part, singing those first few words will cue the group that this is where you're headed and remind them how that part goes.

The key to effectively using sung vocal cues, like everything else, is to practice. You might be playing one chord on a guitar from the end of one section, but the line you're singing as a lead into the next line is on a different chord, not aligned with what you're currently playing for the group.

The secret is anticipation. You hear the next part in your head and, tuning out what the group is finishing singing or your instrument is playing, sing the next phrase before the group has transitioned into that section. You could stop singing the end of the last phrase of the current section (the group by now will know how to end that phrase) in order to take a breath and then start the next section, so you are aligned with the group. This is an effective tool for helping the group keep some fluidity and feel confident that they know what's ahead.

A simpler method is to use your hands or a finger (to point up high for example) *before* the first note of that second higher part, visually alerting the group to sing higher. They need not be musical to know that they should sing the higher note.

The loud sounds of guitar strums can sometimes get in the way of cueing the group vocally. One way to use the strategy of cueing is to stop playing your guitar when you want to cue the next part of the song, so that the group hears your voice clearly and in case what you're cueing is dissonant with the chords you would still be playing in the active line. Since the guitar is just a guide and often the source of rhythm, you can rest assured that if you stop playing for a beat to give a cue with your hand and your voice (and know when to come back in a few chords later), the group will still be able to keep singing without constant guitar accompaniment.

Good vocal technique, particularly as a way to protect your internal instrument from harm due to fatigue or overuse, is worth the investment of time. You need not take ongoing classical voice lessons to learn important techniques over a few sessions about breath support, singing in the right part of your voice, and how to speak to a group while you're singing. It is not uncommon for young songleaders to find they lose their voice easily singing at camp or with large numbers of religious school students in multiple rotations.

Making sure that the keys you select are not overly taxing for your voice, making sure you have the reassuring support of good microphones and a good sound system, as well as considering how others can support you will ensure that your voice stays strong and in healthy shape. You should not shout over groups or sing over talking students. Sing more quietly to get a group's attention, not more loudly. Do not be afraid to speak a tiny bit higher in pitch when you're becoming tired and to breathe more between phrases as you speak. You do not have to sound like a cartoon character; but the lower we speak on our vocal chords, the more tired our voices become. It's important to develop good vocal technique for speaking during particularly taxing times of songleading as well as basic knowledge of how your singing voice works to maintain health and vocal longevity.

Harmony singing is another wonderful way to create cohesive sound in a group. Leading harmony with a partner is not very complicated. One person sings one part, and the partner leads another part. The room setup often will lead to two easy halves of a room, each half led by a partner. If you are alone, it is still possible to create harmony in a group; it just takes practice and different tools.

Sometimes, you can encourage a particularly musical group to add their own harmonies. Many people can hear natural harmony but won't sing it automatically—being afraid to stand out or to disrupt your leadership—until invited. I believe in the power of permission: tell people to feel free to make their own contribution and to live in the singing moments as they desire.

You can encourage the sound of harmony (and invite others to experiment with it) when a group knows a piece extremely well. I will sing a harmony line on top of the group already singing the melody. I might back off of the microphone slightly, so as not to distract them, but so the group hears the harmony and can begin contributing more of it on their own.

Finally, you can teach harmony and lead two parts yourself. If the harmony is important to the song and you'd like to take time to teach a second part to the whole group or part of the group, do so. Wait to do this until the group knows the melody well. This might work best if you have multiple sessions or a long-standing relationship with a group, and you can add harmony after some numbers of repetitions of confident singing of the melody.

If you want a group to carry two parts and you are alone, you must practice moving from one part to the next. Finding the ends of phrases is best, but practice singing the melody of one line and then the harmony of another, and experiment with moving between groups of people. It can be tricky, and your body work will be of great effect here. If there are not two obvious sections of a room but one single group of participants and I want some to sing melody and some harmony, I might sing melody with the group and then raise my eyebrows or tilt my head, move my hand to a different location, and back off the mic a bit for a moment to indicate that I'm singing something different, then lead a bit of the harmony. All the while I'm listening, and if the main part falters, I'll be able to return to that group. This is one of the trickier vocal techniques of songleading and takes practice in different moments to find a style that works for you. Your voice is your primary instrument and your guitar a complement. Having a strong working knowledge of these technical tricks will keep both in shape and put two invaluable resources at your disposal that will come to define your songleading style.

·5·
Know How to Teach

A S DISCUSSED IN THE INTRODUCTION, singing with people often begins with our own love of singing and our love for certain kinds of music (religious, secular, folk, choral, etc.), and that motivation propels us to take the vulnerable steps toward wanting to lead others into that singing. It does originate with our own desires and interests!

And yet, we should always remember that when our goal of communal singing is to serve the community, we must keep in mind who the group is, what they need, and how to invite them into the experience. It cannot be repeated enough: group singing is about the group, not about the leader. This is true even as we are making choices, preparing our material and our skills, and taking risks in front of the group. The power of transformational singing and the moments that move communities, occurs when the group feels ownership of and connection to what they're singing. It's the songleader's job to create that sense of shared commitment and accomplishment.

Introducing something new to a group, in any context, could be called "a teach." It is the teaching of new repertoire or a new melody to familiar words to a group who has not sung it together before. Each of us has to find our own comfort and style for how we teach and how we create buy-in from the group, a willingness to patiently learn new material. Most people do not want to learn new things—or at least when it's framed as work—so they may not be interested from the outset:

- "I didn't come to worship to 'learn' like I'm in school! I want comfort and familiarity!"
- "I thought we were just having breakfast before we moved to the square for the rally. Why do I have to learn a song first thing in the morning?"
- "I'm in school all week. In Sunday school I have to learn about my religion. I don't want to learn a song!"

Given that there might be resistance, before we dive into the mechanics of the actual teaching of repertoire, it's important to consider how we bring the group to the moment of learning. I will lay out some important techniques for teaching songs as a songleader, but with distinctions at the end of the chapter between teaching in prayer settings versus teaching for school or in a community sing.

Experience has taught me that telling the group, "We are now going to learn a song," gives people the opportunity to resist even before you've begun. This isn't about misleading a group, but rather considering why the group might want to know the song you are preparing to teach and sharing that as a way to create openness to working on learning something new.

Many of us learn things unintentionally every day just by being receptive and experiencing things that help us or impact us meaningfully. Only after the fact do we realize that we have absorbed a new lesson. However, if we were told we had to sit down for some "learning" at precisely, say, 1:45 p.m., not many of us would jump at that opportunity.

Use the word "share" in place of "teach." For example, you might say that you would like to "*share* this setting of [liturgical text name]" or say, "As we begin our commemoration of Earth Day, here is a piece about the environment I'd like to *share* with you."

> *Group singing is about the group, not the leader. Consider that in preparing to teach, how you hear a song you know very well in your head is not how the group will hear the song as you teach it. It takes a shift in your thinking to remember or imagine how you once learned the song and its basic structure, and then translate that into how you bring the group along.*

Another option is just to start singing part of the "new" piece or to hum the melody without words. After some heads turn, stop singing and share some context about a given line of text or the concept behind the song. If you have considered your "why" of sharing the piece, then you should be able to tell the group something about who *they* are, why *we* are gathered, and what the piece can do for *us* at this moment.

You don't need to tell them that we're all going to learn a new song, nor do you need to tell them why you love the song. Instead, focus on why this piece matters and suggest that perhaps we will all sing it together.

GETTING STARTED

There is no hard-and-fast rule here about how to approach the very first part of a "teach." What is critical is that you should consider it thoroughly beforehand by asking questions of the piece, of yourself, and of your intention at that moment. This will help guide you toward a desired outcome.

For many who are learning a new song, when given context as it relates to a holiday, theme, concept, or value the group has been learning, the teach will be met with much less resistance. The group will come to see that you're not just teaching something you love (or just making the group work hard), but also that you value and respect their time and energy and are committed to collaborative learning. The depth of meaning that the context brings to the group experience will add to your trust account.

Sometimes, singing the entire song through from start to finish is a good way to begin. You might start with a few sentences about the content or why educationally this is the right piece for the moment and then sing the whole song. This gives the listeners a chance to hear how the whole piece flows, why it matters, and what the potential for singing it can offer. However, I likely wouldn't sing through the whole piece with young children, as they have shorter attention spans and I might want to get right to the singing, with some "repeat after me" time.

For more complicated pieces, singing only a part of the song or at least one time through each section helps a group become familiar with the general flow and sound of a piece before you break down the elements into learnable bites. Other times you want to share just one part of the song, often just the chorus, if it's the most fun part or if it's more complicated. You might sing that chorus through by yourself so the group can hear how it all holds together. And yet at other times you may choose to begin directly with the teach, offering bits of content line-by-line, with no anticipation of where the piece is going.

Once you have sung as much of the song as you feel is right as a way to establish the moment, it is time to move into the technical parts of a teach. I'll lay out the steps here, with the understanding that the nature of a song will dictate that some of these steps can be added to or skipped entirely. As I alluded to earlier and will go into more detail about a little later, the most important part of a teach is not in the teaching but in the listening. Keep that in the back of your mind during this next section.

One of the things to balance in the way you break apart and structure a teach is both what the group needs in terms of their abilities and the structure of the song itself—it's length and complexity, how much time you have (and you may need to teach the song spread over multiple sessions of singing), and the language or text you might need to communicate. All will impact how you design your teach. There are many things to take into consideration when you prepare to teach. The structure of the song (its length and complexity), how much time you have, and what the group needs in terms of content as well as their abilities to be successful, all impact how you design a successful teach.

MELODY AND RHYTHM

Maybe the goal of a particular moment of songleading is not the specific content of a piece, but rather a particular melody or rhythm that is important to what you want to create.

If the melody is the focus of the mood you're trying to create, you may not focus as much on words or of sharing an entire piece, but instead teach with a "la" or "lai" so that participants really learn the melody without words. If you're working on engaging the body, a dance, or the joy found in a very particular rhythm, how you strategize the teach will depend on the tools you have to accent and reinforce rhythm so that the group is in sync with the feeling or motion you wish to create.

You might choose to start with establishing a rhythm by tapping your legs or snapping your fingers. I find that claps are challenging; they are very loud and often drown out the group or the leader. And if the group isn't completely in sync—which is typical—the disorganization of the claps is much more noticeable and distracting than a leg tap or a finger snap.

WORDS

If you are not singing in the spoken language of the group, it's helpful to first say the words out loud. If everyone has visual lyrics available to them, it may not be as necessary, but pronunciation and translation are often useful. Remember, your job is to always be thinking about how to remove barriers to participation for the group you are leading. While there is beauty in origin languages like Latin or Hebrew, people can easily become embarrassed about their pronunciation skills. Take a few moments to help them out.

If you're singing in the vernacular and the rhythm is interesting, it can be a helpful technique to have at the ready a plan to speak the words in rhythm. In English or perhaps even in Hebrew, for example, if the song has a lot of rhythmic syllabic phrasings, you can get "two for the price of one" by having the group repeat the words by speaking without melody, but rather in rhythm. Then, when you add the melodic pitches, the group already has a sense of the flow of the beats.

In the end, words are just sounds that are imbued with meaning through history, tradition, and lived experience. Everybody brings something a little different to the vocabulary. In collaboration with your group, you can add a new layer of meaning to those words, that comes from something you created together in the space.

BREAKING INTO LINES

After moving on from or skipping a teach of the words, you can begin with a standard "repeat after me" format for teaching a song. The general order is that you ask the group to listen first, you sing a piece of the song, and then ask the group to repeat it. Even though this seems easy, there are a few things to consider.

The first is the length of the section of the piece that you'd like to share. How much do you think the group can remember (to listen, then repeat back)? Getting the knack of correctly assessing this takes practice and learning from experience; success and failure as you teach more repertoire over time. Some lines you find may be so short that as you ask the group to "repeat after me" for each short line, it quickly becomes tiresome and tedious. In this instance, the melody is easy enough that you could lengthen the amount that you give to the group. In other cases, the end of the "line" you give them is so far away from the beginning of that line that when they start repeating after you, if there are too many notes, they forget as they move forward.

Here's an example. Let's say that you are teaching Woody Guthrie's "This Land Is Your Land" for the first time to a group who has never heard it. You could choose to begin, "Repeat after me: *This land is your land, this land is my land, from California to the New York island.*" The group starts after you finish: "This land is your land...." But, by "California" and "New York island," they may not remember what you sang earlier.

Or, you could choose to begin, "Repeat after me: *This land is your land (this land is your land), this land is my land (this land is my land).*" But repeating four lines one at a time that are rather simple isn't helpful either.

Because the phrases in the first way are probably too long for a group who has never heard the song before, and the phrases in the second way are too simple and repetitive, my suggestion is to break it up this way: "Repeat after me: *This land is your land, this land is my land (this land is your land…), from California to the New York island (from California…)."*

Pay particular attention to whether the place you plan to stop is a good place to break the flow of the melody. One of the aspects of breaking up a teach that many songleaders forget to consider and to practice is not where to start or stop a phrase, but how getting into the second phrase will work for you, as the leader, and for the group.

The concern for you and the group is how to *begin* the *second* phrase out of thin air. After you sing the second line for the group to listen to, can you start the first note of that *second* line immediately in order to sing with them as they repeat that second phrase? Can you find it in your head or with your instrument? More importantly, can you help the group know where that first note is, maybe before they sing it, so it becomes successful for them? You should not just sing the second line, ask them to repeat it, and then not sing it along with them as they repeat it back to you; they need you to sing as well. If *you* can't find the note to start on for that repeat, the group definitely cannot.

It is unnatural to sing a piece of music from an odd starting place, but it is the nature of the teach. Sometimes when we're nervous about that, our instinct is to sing longer phrases because we don't know how to start in the middle of a line. Often, the group then can't remember all the parts of a very long phrase very well.

Using the above example, we call and receive a response for, "*This land is your land, this land is my land.*" Then we say to the group, "Repeat after me: *From California to the New York island.*" Now, take a few seconds, look around your space, and check your watch just as an exercise. Then, try to start accurately on the note "*from California.*" You as the songleader have to sing with the group on the repeat so that they can get back into that line from the *"New York island"* they just heard you sing alone. As the leader, you are jumping from the last note of *"New York island"* back to the first note of "*from California.*" With practice, you'll be able to pull that off—ending a lovely melodic line when you call it out and immediately starting a phrase on a strange note in the middle, cueing the group to jump in.

It's easy to forget to go back and put line one and two together, or then three and four, and then sew it all together. This is where cueing how that second line comes out of the first will be important.

Once you have strategized how to teach one section of a piece of music (line-by-line or in its entirety if it's short and repetitive), then you have a few choices to make. I suggest singing that part all the way through more than once. That may be where you end, putting those few lines together and singing it enough times that the group feels like they learned a full song. You may not have time to move on to another section. Or the density of that first part may be such that the group is tired, and you move on to the next "part" at another session.

Perhaps one day you learn the chorus, and another day you work on the verse. Or perhaps you move on, using the same strategy (asking yourself how to proceed with each choice): sing the section in its entirety, or go right to the line-by-line teach, working out how to get in and out of middle and end parts.

Ultimately, what all of this comes down to is that you as the song-leader have to be able to sing the song backwards and forwards, in bits and pieces, and with unnatural starts and stops. This takes not just theoretical knowledge ("I can sing it in my head!"), but real practice. Hands on guitar (if you're playing one), standing, singing, starting and stopping phrases at different spots, and practicing alone. Anticipate where the line is tricky or has a funny turn—can you pick up in the middle? How would you cue the note that the group should start on, in order to fix a section with which they're struggling?

As you put it all together, your skills of facial cues, guitar neck movement, using your knees and arms will help remind the group what's coming. This is why we began with the fundamental chapters on full-body songleading and how to use your guitar and voice.

BEING EFFICIENT

Sometimes the first two lines of a song sound the same. Or line three sounds like line one; four like two. To save time, tell the group that these lines sound the same as the first. Or, if only the very last few notes of the line change, then there is often no need to sing the entire line again. But again, starting in the middle of a phrase, tell the group that when we get to the end or to a certain group of words, "we'll just sing this phrase…," and you share only the slightly different notes from where the change begins. This is sometimes called "trimming the fat," as a way to save everyone's time and energy.

Many times verses will sound the same but with new words, or a section will repeat a phrase three to four times. In these cases, there is no need to call and respond more than one time. Just tell the group, "We'll sing it three times. I'll remind you as they come, and then we'll sing the next part."

I emphasize this point here because frequently a group will get fatigued with a teach or want to move on to a more familiar and fun song, not because the new song isn't wonderful or that you're not a good teacher. Rather, it takes too long and it diminishes the energy within the group.

If you can plan a really efficient teach where you don't repeat too much, the group can get to actually singing the whole song through and feeling successful before they'd like the experience to just be over. It's a subtle but incredibly useful technique.

GIMMICKS OR "SCHTICK"

Sometimes our songs have enhancements that either really help the group learn a song, mirror content, or add to the goal of the song. These include movements, physical action, claps, or additional words to fill in spaces. In Yiddish (having made it into the common English vernacular), we call this *schtick*. Schtick is a gimmick—sometimes funny, sometimes not—to add entertainment to a piece. There are different schools of thought about whether schtick has a role in communal singing.

There is no doubt that schtick, in the right context, can be an effective tool. Our instinct, particularly with kids, is to win the group over with something goofy first, particularly if we are not confident that the singing will interest them. I ask you to consider *not* starting your teach with it. It can get in the way of successful singing.

I remember an experience with some fifth graders where the holiday song had accompanying marching, turning, and waving of arms. When it was time to teach the song, I had the youngsters stand up and learn the short march, the turn and lean, and the waving of arms. While they were standing and giggling, I started to teach the song, asking them to repeat after me.

They were not able to sing (or to hear me or concentrate on what I was singing with them) while they were standing and marching. Realizing my error, I sat them down. I then taught the song line-by-line, but I could tell they weren't really listening. They were giggly and full of the energy of the marching. They did get a bit of it, and when I stood to put the things together, they joyfully marched and waved their arms but didn't really sing the song the way I would have liked.

The next time I planned to share that song with a group, I taught them the melody and lyric, seated like any teach, without them knowing there was a dance to come. We then sang it a few times, and when they seemed to really have it down, I invited them to stand up and add the march. With the activity timed to the music they already knew, it became easier to convey the movements. The result was a raucous and joyful song and dance.

All of this said, there are many cases in which the schtick is perfectly in line with the content. My suggestion again is to just be sensitive, tread lightly, and—here it is again—ground yourself in *why*.

In my experience, starting with a clap or a snap with adults can be useful if you need to set a distinct rhythm. An example of this could be at the beginning of a piece about the body or moving, where you could use the body parts perhaps as an entrance to the experience. Or, if there is an element of the song that intentionally uses the body as a way to elevate the mind/prayer/body experience, then it might even be important to begin with the body movement: clapping, slapping the legs, crossing the arms, or whatever physical move is in line with the value and key intention of the song.

Also, the movement or vocal call may help the group remember a Hebrew word or a theological or justice concept. If the repetition of a word in an empty space reiterates a theme or puts a "punctuation" on an idea or a line, it can be useful and fun. Just pay attention to how helpful those claps or callouts are to the learning, so that the schtick does not become the focus of the song.

Overall though, in my experience, songs that add movements as a way to create more energy or appropriately liven up an experience should first be led with the melody and voice, and only later are the motions added as a bonus. Then the movement adds to the fun of singing and even to the goofiness of moving and singing in a space together.

JUST SING THE SONG!

There is another way to approach certain kinds of teaching and singing together, and that's to, well, *just sing*.

Sing the piece over and over again. Give body and vocal cues to help the group just feel the flow of that song by singing it over and over until they hear it and are comfortable lending their voice. This typically works best with a shorter melody, a mantra, a chant, or repetitive refrain.

Sometimes the flow of the repetition not only helps the group learn, but creates the mood and feeling desired in the song, of repetition, of building upon itself. In this way, as more people in the group catch on and the song builds, the moment is efficacious due to the experience of learning this way. These melodies may become awkward if taught too officiously in parts, particularly if the melody is short or designed to flow as one unit.

> *There is no need to tell the group that you're going to teach them a new song or even how much you love that tune. Instead, focus on why the piece matters.*

Worship Setting

Occasionally there may be a melody that will be new for some or all of the worshiping group that will elevate the prayer experience of that particular time and place, and you'd like to "teach" it. Being clear about what you hope the group receives from the piece is essential. Is it important to you that the group sings it perfectly well? I would encourage you to think more expansively about what success might look like in a worship setting as you approach how you teach a new melody in this context. (I highly recommend the book *Leveling the Praying Field: Methods and Melodies to Elevate Congregational Worship* by Merri Lovinger Arian [Transcontinental Music Publications, 2018], an excellent resource on this topic.)

Would you like the group to feel something new? To see the world, those around them, or their own journey in a new light? Would you like the group to make a beautiful sound together as a way to create a collective strength and joy? These will impact if and how you choose to teach within worship.

Introducing new repertoire in worship with intentional songleading choices will help the group feel successful for the prayer or song that will enhance their experience. The key is to adjust your teaching to feel more natural and like part of the prayer experience. Consider how the repetition of a line (with a goal of having the group learn the part) could also feel prayerful, starting quietly and allowing a gentle build of volume or intensity. Perhaps you could say something about the growing sound of our voices or about a concept from that melody that can tie to the connectivity of all of us in prayer. Perhaps you want to maintain the sense of the learning itself being prayer and use some of your body techniques in subtle ways: a gentle head nod to indicate that a group should repeat or that a section is changing, without calling out words or instructions that might take away from the worship. In this way, learning the piece during worship becomes part of the worship and not a dutiful teaching session.

I believe that teaching within worship is incredibly valuable. If there is something new to offer, do not assume that if you sing it they will catch on; on the other hand, the standard techniques for teaching laid out earlier in the chapter are not always appropriate for a prayerful setting. Instead, spend time considering why this new material can enhance the worship and how your prayer leadership can create the environment and invitation for the participants to engage in that new setting in a way that will indeed bring a new experience of holiness or communion to the group.

School Setting

Teaching kids requires the same techniques as those laid out previously in this chapter, but perhaps our lines are shortened depending upon the age of the students and the capacity for remembering long sections. Children love to repeat and to show what they're learning. They also can become easily distracted or tired if the learning is too long and too complex. Consider shortening how much you teach in a single singing session. Children also invest more ownership in a song they help to build or write. Using songs where ideas can be collected from the group to fill in blanks will help kids remember the concepts and ideas because they helped to build and share their own experiences in the creation of the song. Requesting that, as friendly competition, certain sections of the room or rows be in charge of singing a part back to you can create enthusiasm. And so does asking the students to call out to you or remind you of how new parts go, to see what they remember. Teaching students new material should be joyful and fulfilling, not dutiful and taxing.

The most powerful moments with young children occur when you invite students to share their ideas about the planet, the universe, their families, or love. Finding songs that invite honest and creative sharing from young people can create the most fun and deeply transformative singing experiences. Every young songleader should experience the moments when a student shares a powerful story, a memory, or a word that is an honest reflection of what is in their heart, because they were invited to create music together. This is what makes all of the preparation pay off.

We all carry songs with us that we learned in childhood. The power of teaching young children can't be underestimated, and there are many experts who continue to pave the way toward inviting non-pediatric, deep engagement in singing from our young people.

Communal Setting

Teaching new music in a gathering of people who don't usually gather is a powerful way to create an instant connection. When we all learn something together, we feel a sense of unity where one may not have existed before. We can listen and applaud, weep at the tragedy of a moment, or stand shoulder to shoulder holding signs—but until we sing together, we will not feel like one community. A moment that everyone can work toward together provides power and cohesion. Keep your teach simple but deep, accessible but meaningful, and consider using it multiple times in the course of that gathering. It becomes the song of the group and of a moment and will impact the experience greatly.

ॐ

Being a good teacher of new songs is a lifelong skill. No teach is perfect, and no single technique will work every time. But if you can master "the teach," you can be in any space with a plan or with a last-minute song substitution and invite everyone to sing by ensuring that the group learns it and feels empowered to sing it together.

> For more information on teaching, please see appendix C, "How to Teach a Song," page 116.

WE ARE LEADING PEOPLE IN SONG, to sing. This means that the single focus is on the song (even if it doesn't have any words). This does not mean the leader has to be a classically trained vocalist or have the most beautiful voice to listen to. Instead, the leader's voice that is guiding the song must be front and center.

I once attended a Thanksgiving Day communal event at which the songleader's voice could not be heard over the piano and guitar, and so the group did not know where we were in the song. Those who were unfamiliar with the piece were not able to identify the melody to sing along, and we just stood there and watched. When we as songleaders prepare a piece, practice, and go through our plan, the voice should be the place we start from—before we add an instrument or practice with the instrument. We should know the song (melody and lyrics) well and clearly so that our group will easily follow.

What this means in application is that when we lead singing, we start with the song. We will know intricately the melody, the words, the meaning, the mood, and the emotion we want to create with the group singing of that song and what we can do vocally (and with additional tools) to create a group sound that we desire. The song itself is a tool to build community, to accomplish the "why" for that group, at that moment.

Finally, our instrument can be a very helpful and necessary tool. Focusing first on the voice and the song does not mean that a songleader doesn't need good guitar skills, if they use guitar as the prime accompanying instrument. The way we use our instrument as an extension of our body, as rhythmic support for the energy of the song, for assistance with melodic support, or to accent the harmonies a group can build is an important part of songleading with an instrument. How loud or hard we strum and where on a guitar fretboard we choose to support the song instrumentally are choices we make that impact the way the community will respond in the singing moment. This takes practice, deliberate consideration, and honest reflection about our capabilities and whether we have practiced enough to use the instrument to support and even enhance a moment, and not detract from it.

As I mentioned in the introduction, songleaders and the craft of songleading stands on the shoulders of giants, and Pete Seeger, a folk singer and social activist of the last century, is one of them. And yet Pete Seeger was not known as the best vocalist or the best instrumentalist of his day, but he was the best songleader. With banjo, guitar, castanets, or even a cappella, he led small and large groups with his voice, with his vocal cues, and with clear direction to the group. He gave permission and encouraged the group to sing and gave them the confidence to jump in. They were not simply encouraged to listen to his banjo playing.

While we explored how to teach in the previous section (and much of any leading session will include a teach), here we bring all of the ideas shared above into a more cohesive approach to leading a group in general. Some of the ideas below may reference tips for teaching and other times for moving a group through known repertoire.

Here's a helpful tip about doing this work: take good notes. After you lead in any setting, if not immediately then soon after, reflect on what the experience was like. Perhaps ask yourself:

- Thinking about my goals, where did I hit the mark?
- Going through each song, did the group get to where I hoped they'd go? Did they learn the chorus as I hoped, or should I make a note to review it the next time and fix a certain part?
- How was the key/tempo/strum of each song?

Keeping both a list of repertoire for each group or community you sing with and a running catalog of the pieces you lead (with unique information related to each of them) will help you remember adaptations, best keys for certain groups, tricky passages you tend to re-teach no matter how often you teach a given song, and any other pertinent notes to help you strengthen your skills and deepen your tool kit.

MOVE FROM "SINGING ALONG" TO "LEADING"

A common pitfall for a newer songleader is to approach leading singing the same way one would approach being a participant led in song. I have worked with many teen songleaders who will say, "I loved this song when I was in youth group and brought it to my fifth graders in religious school." I then observed them singing (with guitar) that song, the same way they "sing it" in their large teen-energy-filled youth group, in the general direction of the students in a classroom. What follows is not a lot of singing from the fifth grade, just impatient watching. When we approach our songleading simply to relive our own memories and do not translate our experience into how it might be effective or meaningful for others, our leading will fall flat or at worst turn into performance.

The real beginning of songleading as a craft—and of approaching it as sacred work—is to begin to reflect from the outside in and to break down what separates being the one singing in the group from what the group needs in order to be led into song. This is one of the hardest and yet most crucial tasks.

When considering moments that you have loved singing as a participant in a group, stop and ask yourself: What has happened here to help me to know and enjoy that song and to understand my role as the participant? How did the songleader lead the song? Where were they in the room, and who was around them? Did they set their ego aside and lead with their "why"?

I then try to reflect not on how that leader sang the song, but instead on how they led the group successfully in communal singing. Once we can understand the techniques a songleader utilizes to bring people into group singing, we can lead just about any song with practice and careful preparation.

ANTICIPATING CHALLENGE

How do we know what parts a group might find challenging, and how do we anticipate that in our preparation? There isn't a hard-and-fast rule here, but there are a few ways you can feel more prepared to know where the group might struggle or need more support.

You should always test your melodies out with someone beforehand. Even if you are not teaching the song to the group, if you recognize that it's challenging or you're reviewing something the group has learned but perhaps has not internalized fully, knowing where the group will already need some support is helpful. When you run it with someone, try to stop singing as you transition into another part or if the melody moves around a bit. Listen to where your friend is hesitant, stops, or slows their singing (because they are unsure). Based on their reactions, you may be able to expect that the group will struggle there as well.

Try to step back from your own familiarity with the piece. Try to remember where you learned it or heard it. Consider a time when you did not know the piece. Which parts were complicated? Make notes about the times you couldn't remember the chords and always had to look at your chord sheet (indicating perhaps that some change in the music is somewhat counterintuitive) or, even more, when you had to pull out the sheet music to review a portion. If you need to review it, then the group definitely will need to review it as well.

Finally, try to listen while you're singing it with the group. Sing more quietly, listen for where the group falters in volume or lyric. At transition points, just lighten up a bit so you can hear how confident the group is in each piece of the melody. Sure, every group is unique, but making a catalog (as mentioned previously) of how the songs you choose are received, you're setting yourself up for success no matter what happens next time.

ALWAYS BE TWO STEPS (AND STRUMS, BARS, AND PHRASES) AHEAD

When you are leading, very rarely are you simply where you are. Instead you are thinking about the next phrase, even as you sing, cue, and lead the current phrase with the group. In the absence of sheet music (which many cannot read anyway) or of knowing the exact form you would like the song to take, the group is always waiting to receive a cue from you to know what's next.

Try this experiment leading someone in song. Pick a simple song with two parts (A and B), but make it clear that only you will decide whether part A will repeat a second time before moving on to part B. Stand in front of the person (without an instrument), staying still. Sing through part A. The split second that you begin the next section (A again or B) the person you are leading will probably stop singing (unless they randomly guessed the correct part). They will at least hesitate. Or perhaps if, when you began this exercise, you asked them to just keep singing like they were able to guess what was happening next, they likely moved to a different part than you intended and you weren't together.

The group is not in your brain. They have absolutely no idea what's next unless you clearly cue them.

The point of this exercise is to demonstrate that our job as songleader is to always let a group know what is happening next—and to do so before "next" is already here. Not now (we are already in it; the moment, beat, or note has passed the minute you begin to sing it), but next.

This can't be emphasized enough: a songleader can only cue what's next if they are able to be with the group singing in the "now" while at the same time showing, cueing, and projecting what is next at the exact same time. It's like rubbing your stomach and patting your head or walking and chewing gum, except in this case you've added arms, face, and words (maybe in another language), or perhaps an instrument, and maybe even a partner leader!

Being a great singer in the group does not get us ready to just get up and lead a group. It takes craft, art, skill, practice, anticipation, listening, watching, and knowing the content you're leading by heart.

By staying two steps ahead, you can be more in control of the experience—both in your presentation as well as in the group's response and connection.

> *Ensuring that you communicate to the group clearly and that they know what will be happening next will give the group confidence to rise to the task at hand.*

SINGING OUT OF TIME

Sometimes during the teach of a song or when you know something tricky is coming in a more familiar piece, your ability to stretch a line in order to fit in words or drag the singing of certain notes can be helpful. If there is a fast run or a bunch of notes together, until the group knows the song really well, you can stretch them and even over-enunciate them. I wouldn't call it slowing down, because that indicates a distinct tempo shift. Instead, I imagine pulling taffy, where you just stretch a bit and then sort of bounce back into the originally set tempo. Sometimes you don't need to plan to do this but you hear the group falter or have a hard time catching onto a tricky or a fast part, and you can either stretch in the moment or on the next time around anticipate the challenge and pull back just a bit to allow everyone to catch up and catch on.

Stretching time and syllables allows the group to anticipate by watching your enunciation. By giving them time to "hop on" and therefore sing the correct words and notes, you create muscle memory.

I find this strategy helpful with Hebrew liturgical moments, for example, or in a place with a lot of English verse lyrics. We may sing the chorus beautifully, but the verses perhaps have more or less familiar words (because we don't repeat them as often as we do the chorus), and therefore they do not bounce off the tongue as quickly. Stretching time to allow folks to join in will make the experience more pleasurable. While this may seem like a strange and even complicated songleading trick, I use it every time I am in a new situation. When I'm a guest worship leader or teaching a song at a community gathering, I use this technique.

Imagine singing a song on the radio that you mostly know, but not perfectly. If you turn off the radio, you might falter after a few more words or beats. But when you sing along with the radio you're fine. If you were to play back a recording of you singing a slightly unfamiliar song along with the radio, you'd hear that you are just a tick of a beat behind the time of the recorded singer. Not only are you very slightly unsure, but it also takes time for the sound to travel out of the radio, into the car, and for you to hear it, catch on, and join in. Likewise, giving people time to join in is another way that you can connect them to the song and to what you're trying to achieve.

REPETITION

Sometimes if there is a very challenging line that the group repeatedly struggles with, you may need to just sing it over and over again, three, four, or more times to really cement it. This will save time in the long run. Once you've sung one line over and over again, the group will remember it better than any other line in the song!

OVER-ENUNCIATE

Similar to stretching the entrance to a phrase or a phrase itself, you can use over-enunciation as you stretch the time as well. This serves to also allow the group to catch up. Again, if the group is waiting for you and singing even a split second after you, you will never sound together as an ensemble. But they can't always sing exactly with you if they don't know the piece extremely well.

DON'T PANIC, TAKE YOUR TIME!

I once was leading a popular folk song at a community sing event in support of a social justice issue. No one had lyrics in front of them, but the piece was the kind where once you started a verse, people remembered most of the lyrics. The trouble was that I forgot the lyrics to the third verse and had them on a page near but not in front of me on a music stand. I couldn't get there in time to have those first words ready.

I strummed a few extra beats on the final chord and said to the group, "Let's sing that chorus again, it sounded so good!" And while they sang the chorus again, I moved over to the page of lyrics and scanned the page of words until I saw the verse I needed. I turned back to the group, and when that "bonus" chorus finished, I fed the first few words of the next verse to the group.

In similar situations, I have said to the group, as I repeated the chords of the chorus, "I seem to have forgotten the words to the next verse!" Invariably someone (or a lot of people) will know it and begin to sing. Not only do you seem human and approachable in your leading, but keeping your panic at bay and finding a way to solve the problem without worrying that you're off-track will keep that inevitable bungle from derailing the entire singing experience.

If you are leading alone (though you can do this with a partner as well), you have total control over what and when you sing. In other words, there is no rule that says that once you begin a piece, you must sing it exactly as it was written, or without stopping, or as if a metronome were clicking somewhere nearby. If you are leading something that's a standard chorus-verse-chorus-verse road map, sometimes you may find a few things happening:

1. You forget the next verse.
2. You want to say something about a verse before you sing it.
3. You want to sing the chorus again to create more energy before you move on to the next verse.

You have the freedom and permission to hold up, to move a bit out of the simple ABABA flow of the road map of the tune, to keep strumming, and to not keep the time of the number of measures or lines or beats that the song might normally require.

In other words, as you finish a chorus, where traditionally there may be a four-beat strumming pattern before you start the next verse, you could add extra strums to allow you to speak over them, perhaps to say something about the verse (because that verse is important to the theme of the group's experience). Or you could keep strumming a few extra beats (not even a full measure) while you remember the next line or decide a few strums in that you want to sing the chorus again and end the song without that last verse, because you are out of time.

The key, of course, is to cue the group about what to do next, before you expect them to do it with you. For example, if you do decide to repeat the chorus, as you're finishing up those strums, you could say or sing-say the first few words of the chorus to let people know what to sing. You might finish verse three of a four-verse song; you hold a bit, you're thinking about how you're running short on time, and you feed the words to the fourth and final verse or say, "Let's move to that final verse," skipping the chorus in between.

I have seen so many songleaders, right before that shift, rush to force in some words or information so that the downbeat of "one" is still in time with the four-strum pattern that we are "supposed" to play between each part. Whatever they said came out rushed and unintelligible because of a fear of being "late" to the next part. But that's not necessary. Take your time (again if there is not an ensemble relying on a specific chart or arrangement). You have control over the experience you're creating for the group; they don't know the details of your arrangement! They won't know what the exact form is, and that is the magic of live music. As long as you bring the group along with you and make known what you expect from them, you will succeed.

BUILD TRUST

One way to build trust with a group that you are leading is to utilize individual participants in the experience. People love to see themselves in front of the group or participating in a moment of honor or leadership. A participant could be asked to come forward to read something about a piece you will be singing or answer a specific question that can lead into that moment. Maybe others in the group play instruments (they could be asked to bring them in advance), or someone may not play but you invite them to tap on a drum, lead some clapping or hand motions, or hold up a page with lyrics or a picture. If you are leading a two-part round or a piece with a clear second harmony on top, you could ask someone to lead the other half of the group in a counterpart line. The more relationships we create with participants, the more likely they are to join us wholeheartedly in singing.

Worship Setting

Leading singing in a worshiping space takes those same skills but a different intention—a different why. We ask ourselves: What would success look like? Does it matter if everyone gets all the words correct? Are there some moments where what we sound like and accuracy matters, and others where they do not? Do we want the group to feel full and strong, or do we want to allow for the still small voices from within to hum gently in each person? These ideas will dictate how you lead—how you use your body, the words, and the supportive instruction you give to the group throughout the worship.

If you have a guitar, many of the same techniques apply to cueing the group. Many folkier worship melodies or ones without a hymnal or songsheet as a guide will have an A and a B structure, and in this case, using the neck of your guitar to cue the group gently can be a useful tool. The head, face, and arms can be particularly useful during worship, probably more than vocal cues or "callouts." Those run the risk of disrupting the prayer flow or the mood or spiritual language of a given moment. Instead, a nod or a head lean and raised head and eyebrows can indicate what might happen next without having to shout out a lyric. Stretching certain phrases or words, particularly if not in the vernacular language of the group (like Hebrew), can also be helpful if there is a long prayer text.

Sometimes in worship, if you have someone who offers a reading or a spoken frame before you are to begin a melody, playing a bit of the melody or a gentle strum indicating the feeling of the prayer or moment on the guitar can create the appropriate ambience or segue from what is being taught to lead into the melody. This might minimize the feeling of a casual song session. If you play a long introduction on your guitar after the reader ends, the group not only becomes passive, but is watching you perform or lead, and the sense of a group worshiping as one might be lost.

At the same time, not every piece should underscore reading. Create intentional moments that work for you and your community. If everything has a musical undertone, the entire experience can have a sameness or a drone-like feeling that may prevent moments of joy, of true silence, or of letting an idea or reflection sink in.

School Setting

Schools create singing moments as ways to teach concepts, create community, and learn meaningful ways to build something in a group. Most schools will require some amount of curricular support or content reinforcement. Leading young people in singing is a valuable experience, and having the skills to know where the group needs to go, being aware of where the students are emotionally and spiritually, and utilizing the staff and space in supportive ways will allow you to have wonderful music experiences with young people. Remember that the teachers and additional staff can be songleading partners—even if they don't lead singing. They can sit with students, help with hand motions or words, direct attention to you, or run interference if the group is too rowdy. And even if you make mistakes, they can be fun opportunities for you to be corrected or ask for help from a student, allowing them to shine.

Communal Setting

Gatherings of groups to celebrate communal events, civil activities, or justice actions often require music. To lead musical moments in them can be quite powerful. The keys are to stay true to the intention of the group, to know who the group is and where they need to be, and to find repertoire and context settings that allow for everyone to feel seen and acknowledged in their space. Sometimes the space, the sound, or the logistics are messy, but if you have focus on the meaning of the moment, communal singing can change the outcome of any gathering.

ॐ

These are all tricks that are crucial to helping a group stay together and continue to build trust with the group. We may wonder, "Why does it really matter if the group is perfectly together? We're not a choir or professional singers." The reason it's an important strategy for group singing is that it gives the group confidence. By leading them with intention and planning, you are creating a safe space for vulnerable singing where the group doesn't feel misled or alone in the unknown.

Conversely, if it feels too hard, if there is too much "work" for the group that doesn't seem to pay off, or if no one is together, then it will not achieve your goal of creating a sense of group, of being together, and of our ability to raise our voices, with confidence, in song. We should feel free and able to raise our voices out to the world.

Leading songs (not just singing songs you love) requires a big shift in preparation, planning, and presence. You will know that you've made the shift when you feel that you have moved from a lover of songs to someone leading others. You will be able to transition or change direction after you notice something the group needs and then react to it. These are the moments that truly matter.

BEING A SONGLEADER IS A BUSY JOB. Before you even get up to sing, you have to do homework to make sure you know what you're getting into and why. When you get going, you have to be thoughtful about tempo, the physical cues you're giving the group, how they're reacting, and quite a few other things.

In addition to all of this, I want to suggest that you should always be listening. The songleaders who get the strongest response are those who are able to read the mood of a room, who are tuned in to those who might be presenting the song with them (like a partner or band), and of course, who are keeping tabs on that inner voice as well.

LISTEN TO YOUR INSTINCT

When you sit alone preparing a music session and laying out the goals and metrics of singing with any given group, imagine what it is to be a participant in the session. As you consider how to use instrumentation, what key to sing in, or how you might lay out a teach, trust your instincts as a leader and continue to call back to what it is like when you are a participant in an excellent song session. Call to mind teachers, mentors, and coaches—and imagine how they might structure such a moment. When you begin to practice and prepare for leading, trust that you have done all the necessary preparation, that your motivation and goals are clear, and that you will have the tools you need in the moment.

When you are at last in front of a group, let go and listen to what your gut tells you. If you feel that something hasn't been clear, trust that, and stop to make a pivot. If you think that the setting isn't conducive to the set list you planned, trust that observation, have faith that you will be able to make a shift, and do so. Your instinct as a leader will often be correct if you have started with many of the tools used to create successful group singing.

Of course, sometimes what you imagine might be successful in the planning of a teach doesn't go as well as you had hoped. This is where it's important to listen and, soon after your session is over, to make notes for yourself about where the tricky spots were and where the group seemed to lose the flow.

Perhaps at your next session you can jump right into the tricky parts with which the group seemed to struggle from the first teach, before you start to sing. Or you can review the parts that were a bit messy in order to create more chance of success. For example, you might say, "Today let's start where we left off last time. We all were a bit confused. Let's spend a little time to fix that part so we can put it all together beautifully today!"

LISTEN TO YOUR PARTNERS

Dan Nichols, one of my partners in songleading work for over twenty years, and I still sit with each other before a particularly important or difficult teach and ask each other questions. "Should I sing the chorus all the way through, like this, or just jump in line-by-line? What about these two lines together—did that feel like too much?" Yes, we have a shorthand born of years of working together, but we never take the privilege of being able to lead a group together for granted.

Having a partner or a coach, someone with whom you can road test your songleading, is a wonderful way to prepare. As my partners and I continue to learn and grow in our work we find that having mentors and accountability partners to run ideas by, to test leading techniques, and to ask for regular feedback has been invaluable to our own growth as songleaders and teachers.

I often find myself imagining what a respected colleague would do in a given moment, perhaps as the group appears to be bored or is struggling with a part. I watch them intently when I am a participant in their leadership, and I learn and observe their technique, shifts, corrections, body language, and more. This is a crucial attribute of a great songleader—one who, when they are being *led* by others, sees it as an opportunity to watch and learn.

Partners are important. Even if you aren't with them, you can call their work to mind to reinforce your own work.

LISTEN TO THE GROUP

This is where serious listening takes place: live and with voices all around you. It is difficult and requires dedication and focus. You have prepared with a partner, road-tested a melody, and thought through presentation strategies, and you are now standing in front of a group. A number of things can happen.

You can lead as prepared and finish, then reflect to yourself. "That went well! I hit my marks, I led as planned, I remembered the cues and the reminders. I did it!" Hopefully this happens frequently. Almost always, though—no matter how well things go—there are things to learn, reflect upon, and shift for next time.

"What am I listening for?" is a common concern. The question that many songleaders are not always able to answer fully is how the group experienced the teaching of a new piece. You might be able to say, "The group had fun—I think they got it." The question is, how do you know for sure? You could wait until the next time you are together and begin to review the new piece and see how much was retained. This is a useful strategy.

But I encourage songleaders to ultimately feel so prepared and comfortable in what you're leading that you are able to have more than half of your focus on the group and what is happening for them in each moment.

> *You might be able to say, "The group had fun—I think they got it." The question is, how do you know for sure?*

You should also be keeping an ear out for inaccuracies. The only way to know if you will need to repeat a line again (and maybe multiple times) is if you can hear, see, or sense that the group didn't get it the first time. A colleague of mine has been known to gently and in a friendly way chide the group when he hears those inaccuracies, saying, "You're composing!" You can have them repeat after you, and if you are just going through the motions of a "repeat after me" line-by-line teach and you don't notice that they did not really sing the line back to you with accuracy or confidence, then the song isn't really taught.

Instead, if the group repeats and they trail off at the end of the line or seem to stumble and mutter, it's your job to say, "Let's try that again! First, I'll sing...Now you try again."

Try singing the line a bit slower, as we discussed in the teach section. Or if you really heard where the group got confused, you can isolate those small bits and repeat just that phrase. If you don't hear the tricky parts for the group and fix them along the way, the piece will never take off or you'll find that you're always fixing a little bit here and there.

Eventually the group will communicate that they don't "like" the song, when the truth is that they just never learned it well and so it became frustrating to sing. That's no fun.

Listen for whether the group is struggling to reach certain notes. The question of what keys work best in groups is a complicated one, and there is no hard-and-fast rule. There are good places to start in your planning, but if your goal is successful communal singing, listening will always give you the best judgment.

Many artists and communal singers will say that melodies that range from between middle C and C on the staff are the best bet for communal singing. Generally speaking, in my experience, A below middle C is at about the bottom and the C or D on the staff are about the high point of the range. Some pieces work with low notes (for low singers or to create a grounded, warm, and quiet sound) and some with high notes (either lightly for effect or loudly for energy).

When choosing a key, first consider what you can reasonably sing to feel confident in your voice and to have the ability to communicate the piece effectively. Occasionally you might need to jump an octave but encourage the group to sing somewhere else, but that's rare. That might be necessary if you are teaching or leading a three-part piece where you might not be able to sing all the parts, but you can teach the group to sing them. While we all have different voices and comfort in different ranges, we need to be able to sing strongly and often for extended periods of time, so vocal care is important.

Figuring out where the group should be singing, what you hope the song will sound like, and what ambiance or mood you hope to create with the piece takes critical listening and the willingness to pivot if necessary.

For example, if a certain piece occurs at the high point of a session of singing and you want big energy, a slightly higher key will help. If the group sings too low, they can't provide lift in energy or voice. While you of course do not want people screaming or straining, a piece that you previously taught in the key of C or might sing on a Sunday morning in C, you might sing in the key of D at the end of a program of singing or at a celebration or festive retreat.

Perhaps the mood you want to create is gentle and light. Perhaps you sing low so it's warm and no one pushes, or you sing a bit higher and a bit lighter on the voice. Maybe you want the chorus to be comfortable because it is the most repeated, has the most hooks, and is a place to call "home" in the song, so if the verses are too high or too low, it's a worthwhile sacrifice. These are all things to experiment with and consider.

You won't know for sure until you are with a group, and then you *listen*.

LISTEN...TO EACH OTHER

Finally, part of the magic of songleading comes when the group is able to hear one another and to listen to the power of the sound they can create with one another. Ideally, you don't want the group only listening to you or only worrying about getting it correct (after all your focus on accuracy and inclusive teaching).

To experience the power and life-changing moments of group singing, the participants must be able to actively listen to each other. Joey Weisenberg, a teacher and leader in communal singing, says with regards to creating space and moments of quiet and silence that "...a singing community is really a listening community," (*Building Singing Communities*, Hadar, 2011, page 16). He reminds us that our work is not just about making sounds from our mouths but listening to what others are contributing and being aware of the beauty we can create together. Our confidence builds, our voices strengthen, and the commitment to the idea of what we are doing together matters when we can hear each other building a holy sound.

ONE OF THE MOST REWARDING SONGLEADING EXPERIENCES is to lead alongside a colleague. And part of the reward, in addition to feeling less alone in the work, is the opportunity to trust and be trusted by someone else in the communal songleading craft. Songleading with a partner adds more fun to your work—like having someone help you clean up at recess. The work is always easier when we do it with others!

Having someone to plan with may help keep the goals alive as you discuss choices, allows for a variety of leadership, and often expands your repertoire. Sometimes a piece might be great for the group but it is better led by your partner and not you—if you were alone you might not choose it, but with this teammate this great choice can become part of your programming. In a large space for singing, many songleaders together may allow the participants more access to the music and the leadership.

Diversity of leadership also helps, as it allows different voices, styles, personalities, and identities to invite the group to engage in singing. Many participants are aided by seeing or hearing something that feels similar to their own style or identity. Mixing diversities of vocal style, gender, with instrument and without, energy, and style of songleading can add more choices and therefore more diverse ways that music might be presented to a group.

Of course, there are challenges and work to be done in creating a strong songleading partnership. Any of the benefits above can also become a hindrance or create unintended complications if not thought through carefully in advance. Building a relationship and doing the work of planning (which will take more time than if you were alone) are necessary to create successful partnered songleading.

One of the common misconceptions about leading with a partner is that your communication back and forth between each other has to be ongoing and that you must be together all the time.

Often in songleading work with young people and busy schedules like a camp or school, preparation time is very limited. I have coached many young songleading teams who spend a lot of time practicing every song together, looking only at each other to make sure everything is in sync and working out exactly how many times to play through a given part. Often, all the time is spent playing through everything together and not doing other kinds of planning, like working on your own chords and words, preparing language to introduce a moment, and researching more about the group, the space, and the goals of the experience.

Playing through and making sure you're in sync is not the best use of time, even though that might appear counterintuitive. Furthermore, playing through everything to perfection is not the way to lead clearly and efficiently with the group, and it can set you up for failure.

What happens if one of the songleaders forgets the plan? Or, as is a must in songleading, what if one member of the team is listening to the group and wants to be able to adjust to where the group is? How do they effectively shift?

This dilemma gets us to one of the most important parts of co-leading, which may be a bit of a contradiction: only one person leads at a time; only one person is on point for each piece. Our instinct when we partner would be to share—to lead together. Unfortunately, two simultaneous leaders of a song rarely works. Instead, the songleader who is on point should be the primary leader of the piece.

Try to imagine two people telling you the same story at the same time or reading from the same children's book. Each may use a different voice, read faster or slower, or pause for effect or to see if the group is laughing at the jokes at different times. It would be hard to follow the story if two people were reading it together. The same is true for songleading.

Two people can "lead" when you are singing together; there are more instruments, more energy, and more people to move close to folks, particularly if the group is big (and we want to get close). But only one can actually make the decisions live in the moment. You will work together on the general plan and frame, and both of you should be on the same page. But once you're leading, the group should know clearly who the one person will be whom they can trust to follow. As most of the time you will be leading more than one song, you could plan to alternate. Or each leads the pieces that work most to your own strengths. Consider voice style and range, tempo or vibe, and text or lyric.

Having a partner in a secondary position follow the leading partner is also incredibly helpful. The second songleader can model for the group how to support, learn from, and follow the leader. For example, if you and I are working together and you are teaching a song, I want to cause as little distraction as possible. I want the group to focus on you so that they get clear instructions. Facing you, I might crouch in front of the group, and then help the group when it's time to repeat after you. When I focus my attention on you, people who look at me will see me following *you* (and not looking at them or leading a small group of singers accidentally in another direction). I can help by singing loudly near the group as another anchor of the melody. I know the song, but I'm going to act as a semi-participant but who knows a bit more and can help the group along.

> *Co-leading is most effective when only one person leads at a time. Only one person should be on point for any given song.*

The hardest part of being the secondary songleader who knows the song as well as the leader is waiting patiently and truly letting your partner lead. This means not only refraining from making known any choices you might make but that your partner makes differently, but also training yourself to wait and allow them to lead both the group *and* you. In this way, if they lead you correctly, you will be a better support to the group.

Here's an example. I was once one of three songleaders spread out in front of a hall, standing on the floor, where people were seated stadium style in rows that were slightly horseshoed. We moved around a bit as we sang, in order to make contact with and get close to people farther back in the hall. *[See figure 15.]*

I was not on point for a particular folk song that was a simple A and B song, but sometimes the song's design led to a repeat of the chorus—part A—before the return to part B. So it might look like ABABA in one song session and AABAABAA during another gathering.

I was standing down a side aisle, and the person on point for that song was in the middle but far enough away that I could not hear her voice. I also only heard loud voices of participants near me, singing along robustly. As we ended the first part A, I intentionally stopped play-

LEADING WITH PARTNERS MEANS THAT FOR EACH INDIVIDUAL SONG, ONLY ONE PERSON IS "ON POINT" AT ANY TIME.

LEADING FROM THE FRONT, THE LEADER CUES THE OTHER SONGLEADERS AS MUCH AS THE GROUP.
THE OTHER SONGLEADERS ALWAYS TURN TO CHECK IN WITH THE LEADER, WHO MAKES THE DECISIONS.

Figure 15

ing my guitar on the last line, turned to find the leader, and even stood on my tiptoes to be able to see her.

As we came to the end of the line, folks near me followed my eyes toward the leader as well. She too stood on her tiptoes, lifted her guitar neck, turned to face me, and the third songleader, who was on the other side of the room also leaning toward the leader and playing his guitar very quietly, called out the lyrics for part A again and began that section. I sang along with the leader and then was able to rejoin the guitar strumming, singing part A again while turning to connect with the section of the group I was closest with. My rule of thumb is, as you come to the end of *any* single section, you check in with the person on point to see where the next section might come.

The beauty in this songleading experience was not only in the clarity that occurred for the group, but of a partnership based on learning from each other and supporting each other. This is what makes for deep and meaningful songleading partnerships, and the three of us found leading together rewarding.

Worship Setting

Worship co-leading is dynamic and really depends on the nature of the worship and the type of clergy or prayer leadership in the congregation. Similar thinking also applies to leading singing in worship; one person takes the lead to set the tone, tempo, and introduction of a piece. Perhaps then other leaders sing along and support the leader, serving as a mirror or model for the group.

Sometimes challenges arise. A very zealous leader may be so caught up in the spirit of the hymn, song, or blessing that they speed up or sing louder than the assigned leader. This is not uncommon, and while it is sometimes frustrating, there are a few choices one has. Most often, in the moment it's worth just continuing on with your plan. As long as the other leader really isn't taking the group off course, it's usually best to let them sing along. Their enthusiasm could be contagious.

If it verges on becoming a distraction, you can rescue the moment by leaning into it. You could say, for instance, "Reverend/Rabbi so-and-so is going to lead us for now. They sure are passionate about this moment. Let's let their spirit lead us!"

At the conclusion of the worship, it's worth speaking with your leading partners. Asking questions might be a helpful way to open the conversation. "How do you think [a particular moment] went today? Were we successful in what we hoped to achieve?"

Maybe they will say that they didn't notice the group or that they thought it was great, while you experienced the group as passive and confused. You shouldn't be shy about suggesting that you observed or experienced something else. Trust is built in positive situations as well as in difficult ones.

Find a way to praise or offer support while offering constructive feedback. "They really liked you and wanted to honor you, but I think they also were trying to follow my lead. We were so much in that holy moment that it got away from us! If you don't mind, next time perhaps let me sing a little bit and set the tone and tempo before you jump in?"

We've all seen two people announce two different page numbers, and we all laugh. Ultimately, only one of the page numbers was correct. The same applies here. One leader with many participants, co-creators, and partners.

School Setting

In a religious school setting, having other leaders is helpful to engage with different parts of a group. It is particularly nice to be able to roam to different parts of the room to invite young people to sing who are on the periphery and feel disconnected or who may be distracted by things that aren't on the program for singing. In both cases the proximity of a songleader can help get them back on track.

Another way to think about partnered leading is to think about who in the community could join you in front to help "lead" a song. Is there someone who could help with claps or movement once the melody has been established and you're ready to include some additional fun? Are there a few students who are having trouble focusing, so being in front with you and co-leading will keep them from finding inappropriate ways of disengaging? Leading songs with multiple easy parts where students could lead one section in one line or creating a special movement with part of the group is a nice way to lead with partners as well.

Sometimes any of these problems might be solved by having a student or perhaps the teacher co-lead with you. Students often enjoy that, and it can make them feel more connected to the song.

Communal Setting

Having more than one singer, leader, or vocalist is very helpful when you are involved in a community event, march, or gathering. The rule still applies that only one person is on point, but everyone can lead. When walking or marching, the other songleaders can spread out in the group—still making sure they can hear or see the leader—and help spread the enthusiasm to other parts of the group, particularly those a bit farther from the front or wherever the leader is stationed.

Consider that if a group of leaders is spread out in a crowd, you should go into the event with the expectation that you will *not* be together. Be forewarned: singing outside is very difficult. The sound travels up and has no bounce or reverberation that contains the sound and brings clarity to a group. Therefore, if you are in a march, different leaders can be spread out to create singing and connection in different points along the way—but will likely not be in sync with other leaders.

For example, the leaders might have a set repertoire they'd like to use, or they know they have a set in their back pocket, but they keep a loose plan as they lead the people with whom they're marching. This also will allow for the likely possibility that someone else marching near you might have a song and start singing as well. The whole experience can feel more shared and more egalitarian.

⚭

A good songleader works in concert with everyone involved in the experience, from planning to setup to presentation. Bringing with you a collaborative spirit and a willingness to share the stage means that the group will benefit from the whole being greater than just the sum of its parts.

Know Your Repertoire

NOW THAT WE HAVE ALL OF THESE SKILLS SET and we continue to evolve as we gain experience songleading, it's finally time to talk about repertoire. While it may seem like this is the most important thing, it shouldn't be collected until you've considered what goals you want to achieve and after asking many questions of yourself and your partners and team about what success would look like, and the space and sound, about where the participants are coming from and going to.

Repertoire matters deeply. Now that our songleading skills have been improved, the content of the singing will affect the feeling and mood of the group. It will change what they take with them when they leave and how they see themselves and their world a little differently than before they started singing together.

There is no right repertoire, but here again thoughtful preparation will create successful group singing.

I tell songleaders who are newly hired at a camp, in a school, or for worship that they need not learn every piece the group already knows. Sit with people who have either songled there before or with core leaders to gather a repertoire list and to create a separate, short list of core pieces. These pieces should be ones the groups sing often and love. The new songleader can be set up for success by having a small repertoire that they know very well, as opposed to vaguely knowing lots of pieces, but not well enough to lead. That newer teacher or songleader can get up to partner-lead those very well-known songs and then sit out to learn with the group other parts of the less familiar repertoire. It is not helpful to learn an entire chordster or songbook from start to finish. Find a few pieces, set some deadlines, and work them up incredibly thoroughly.

Most of our repertoire ideas will come from the group. Asking questions about what they know, where they've been, and what makes up the community will help you create a repertoire of familiar material. To find other material, I suggest finding other leaders of music who have worked with that group or know the style or experience of the group in order to collect ideas for new pieces.

Sometimes you hear a piece in a secular environment, concert, playlist, or show and find yourself singing along or the message moves you. Keep a digital or physical notebook to jot down song ideas—including not just the title or composer/artist but what you felt when you heard it and what message you thought emerged from the piece. Then when you are preparing to be with a group and there's a request for a certain theme or concept from the organizers, you can refer to that list to remember a lovely new piece you heard that you would like to learn to share with the group at just the appropriate moment.

All of the pieces you know will not stay in your head forever! Allow time to practice. You may have known a song for more than a decade, but if you don't sing it to lead it often or you haven't put fingers on your guitar for that piece in a while, then allow time for review. Countless times (essentially before every service I lead while on the road), even if I'm selecting pieces I know well and lead all the time, I play through everything a few times. I prefer to lead mostly from memory. In order to be focused on the group, to be listening to them, and to be present with them (and not lost in a lead sheet), I refresh my memory about song form and chords, then select the best key. "I was sure I always sang this in C minor—but that sure seems high now. Ah yes, A minor is best!" It's best to prepare all of that, even with long-familiar melodies, than to begin and assume that you remember which key to play in or how the verse goes ("I've been singing this song forever!") and have it elude you.

BACK POCKET SONGS

You will need a repertoire of songs that experienced songleaders call "back pocket songs." Back pocket songs are pieces that you not only know by heart and need no preparation, but are part of a file of songs in your head that you can fall back upon when you have to pivot in any of the three settings (worship, school, and communal). Every songleader should have at least five pieces of music for playing with guitar and five that you can lead a cappella that will work on most occasions in which you may find yourself working.

For example, do you have a few song settings that are key to your faith and that come with built-in power and meaning? I had a rabbinic partner once who was delayed coming to worship because of an emergency. I had a few extra worship-appropriate opening pieces that I could lead with the group while we waited for him to arrive. Another time, my accompanist had to leave in the middle of a service for an emergency, and we had planned a song about peace, featuring her piano accompaniment, that I could not play on guitar. I was still ready and able to lead the group with the same intention either on my guitar or a cappella because I had two or three other peace songs in my "back pocket" that I was able to share.

In fact, the need to fill time is a common occurrence. You may receive a sign from the back of the room to drag out the session or you may need to fill five or ten more minutes before the speaker arrives or before the kids can go back outside after a storm. I have also been asked to lead a group spontaneously when I did not have my guitar with me. I could lead a connecting piece, or something fun and light.

The back pocket songs that are best are ones that do not require a song sheet or a projection of words (when the group has few barriers to entry). Here are a few suggestions to fill your back pocket with flexible song options:

- Rounds: easy two- or three-part rounds where folks can be separated into groups.
- A song with body motions, clapping, or sounds that groups can make easily (as I said earlier, sometimes schtick can be useful!).
- A song using call-and-response or a song where participants have to call out words or phrases or ideas to fill in along the way.
- A "sing-down" with kids: Break the group into four, assign a topic to each, and ask them to come up with songs about that topic. Have them share in a round-robin style until the groups run out of ideas.
- Songs of secular folk tradition or songs that may be already part of a popular canon with the group.

Concerning songs that are generally well-known or popular, we often assume everyone in a group will know a song like "This Land Is Your Land" or an oft-heard pop song. But not everyone does. People come from different parts of the world and from varying faith traditions, with unique experiences and access to the melodies and themes of the place and space in which you live. By listening and being in tune with your group, you can ensure that something you intended to be inclusionary does not become exclusionary.

NEW REPERTOIRE VERSUS OLD REPERTOIRE

The question of new repertoire is one that's often on the minds of songleaders. All musicians and singers love to learn new things and love the feeling of bringing a new idea or sound to a group of people. The desire to share new discoveries with the groups with whom we sing runs strong in most songleaders.

I am not disparaging the seeking out and sharing of new repertoire. I value it greatly for myself as a songleader and for the power new melodies have with a group.

But there are a few things to think about when it comes to how you select repertoire (new or familiar). In Jewish tradition, at the turn of the twentieth century Rav Abraham Isaac Kook wrote, "The old will be made new, and the new made holy." Let's start there.

We often believe that groups are sick of the same repertoire. That is not always the case. More often than not, it is *us* who are more tired of what is familiar. The group not only doesn't find those melodies as repetitive as we do, but the familiarity actually brings them comfort. There can be great power in a group singing something with ease, at full volume, where they can enjoy the success of their sound. Let the feeling of the group be the focus and rather than working to get something new "correct."

There are a few things you can do with familiar repertoire to keep it fresh and alive for the group:
- Be thoughtful about where you place it in your set. After a teach or review of something new, something very familiar to the group can lift them with relief and the joy of singing something comfortable.
- Slightly alter the key, the arrangement (starting with the second part first), or the voicings (the way you play chords on the guitar) might give an old tune new life and also give the group an opportunity to hear it in a different, more intimate way.
- Change the tempo. Something that is always wildly fast and has lost its meaning could be given a lighter groove for an easier sing

(change the key as well—it will keep it a bit slower if it's a bit lower).

• Teach the group a harmony part to the piece that could enhance it.

• Find a new way into the song by how you talk about it. Could someone in the group share an experience that connects to the song? Can you tell a story (personal or found) that links to the meaning of the song? Is there something in the world or the community in which you're singing that would be a powerful link? Often, it's context that colors a song and breathes new life into it.

New songs, melodies, and interpretations of other hymns and texts are written every day. Very often we are moved as we walk through the world hearing something that opens us up in new ways. We want to share that experience with the group.

Our instinct when we are excited about a new piece is to bring it to a group and tell the group how much we love the song and can't wait to share it. Occasionally our relationship with the group will be such that their trust in us is enough, and they'll be pleased to learn a new song simply because we love it. But that's rare.

> *When you consider new repertoire that you hear and that inspires you, remember that it's not about the song, but rather how it fits and needs to be tailored for any number of groups with which you sing. While we might think that finding the perfect song will solve our problems, the success of the song has as much to do with its context, goals, space, and people involved as it does with the song itself. Did you start the repertoire selection process with the "why?"*

As I've mentioned throughout the book, our goals for songleading and for singing with a group should not begin with what the great songs are that we want to share. Find your "why" and share it with the group. They will respond best to why *this* song in *this* moment.

It doesn't matter to them when you learned a song or how new it is. Instead, they want to know that your reasons for sharing that piece are for *them* and not for you. If you find something in the meaning, the rhythm, or the way it will sound in the group's voice as a way to invite the group to sing it, you will be successful.

What might we consider when we are reviewing repertoire that might work with a specific group? Here are a few ideas that might stimulate your thinking as you prepare and can be used as prompts for how you would share that repertoire with your group:

- I find this song useful when I'm feeling _____.
- As we approach this holiday/sacred time/gathering, the _____ idea from the _____ text helps us focus on what this time can mean to us.
- When I'm feeling stiff or stuck in my body, singing this song and moving to the song's beat gets me going. I hope it does for you as well; let's try!
- When we hear about [any topic] in the news, singing a song of peace or of hope allows us to feel buoyed to keep working for a better world, even when it feels so hard.

PLANNING THE "ARC" OF A SESSION

When you're planning for a session of singing (outside of worship), it's useful to consider the energy of the group. Similar to the pacing of a novel or a film, the energy arc of a song session matters. It would not be helpful to a group to get everyone on their feet with a very fast jumping- and clapping-heavy "jam" kind of piece and then ask everyone to chant quietly on a few harmonized notes. You may think that would be the best way to move the group forward, but if you watch and listen in group settings (not just children and teens, but adults as well), it's not always easy to come down from high energy to a very sweet focus. We feel full of excitement, of adrenaline, and we want to chat and share our joy and enthusiasm with our neighbor. It will be challenging to try focusing by sitting still and closing our eyes.

A basic songleader arc you could start with is the bell curve. *[See figure 16.]* You can utilize the bell curve in either direction. Many singing sessions with kids in a school or teens in a youth group are designed around this model. You start loosely with an even tempo and relaxed melody (not bottom energy, but close to middle energy) and then build your way perhaps to a peak moment of energy, familiarity, or joy.

Often a good place for a teach is at the very beginning, when everyone is fresh, or after the first gathering. Start with an even-tempoed song to get everyone centered, and then share something the group can learn together. Then follow that teach with a familiar "reward" song.

STARTING WITH SLOWER MELODIES, THIS BELL CURVE RISES TO A HIGH POINT AND THEN COMES BACK DOWN.

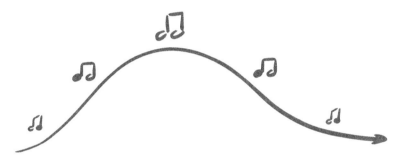

Figure 16

After the gathering song and teach, the energy could build a bit higher with something familiar but more upbeat, leading to a high point. Perhaps that high-point piece is something familiar that you do in many settings, and here, as it's the top of the arc, try pushing the key a tiny bit higher than usual in order to keep the energy high. You don't want to jump into the slow songs just yet. You could move into something with some movement, but not as high as the highest point; you slowly bring the group back down to some more mellow singing. Perhaps the arc ends lower than where you began or ends mid-tempo and nothing really slow happens at all. It's up to the needs of the group and your goals.

Conversely, if you want the group to experience more mellow singing, harmony time, or gorgeous drawn-out slow melodies, you could flip the arc: start mid-tempo and gradually slow to a warm, slower place in the flow, and then maybe bring the energy back up—not too wild, but to a mid-tempo to propel people to their next activity. *[See figure 17.]*

Other possible designs of your session are a straight line upward or starting high and working your way down. *[See figure 18.]* You do not have to teach near the beginning, but be aware that the more the group sings together and the higher the energy is, the more challenging it is to teach the group—particularly something with lots of words or with a complex message. A quick call-and-response song would work, but the more the group gets loose and relaxed, the more challenging a teach can be.

Remember that a lot of the planning of the shape of the arc is dependent on where your group has been and where they are going. If the students are moving toward nap time or rest hour, an arc that starts low and ends at the raucous jumping song might not be appreciated by the staff in charge of nap time. If your group is heading out to the ball field or for a special competitive game outside, you want to build them toward energy and enthusiasm. This is where all the research you will have done about your group will affect how you design the repertoire flow (in terms of tempo and energy) into a deliberate arc.

After you consider these concepts, you can fine-tune the repertoire for the particular venue in which you'll be working.

Worship Setting
Repertoire for worship is a subject worthy of exploring in an en-

STARTING MID-TEMPO, OR UPBEAT (BUT NOT VERY-HIGH ENERGY), THIS INVERTED BELL CURVE BRINGS THE GROUP DOWN TO MELLOW SWEET SINGING AND THEN BACK TO MID-TEMPO AGAIN.

Figure 17

IN THIS SONG SESSION, YOU START LOW AND BUILD TO THE HEIGHTS OF RAUCOUS SINGING!

WITH THIS ENERGY, YOU START HIGH AND BRING THE GROUP DOWN TO ENI MELLOW AND QUIET.

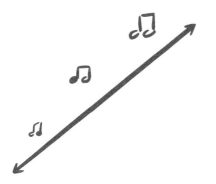
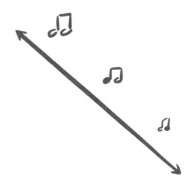

Figure 18

tirely separate volume. As every praying community is different in denomination, faith, history, and legacy, as well as differing in access to trained musical clergy or ministers of music, it is impossible to dictate best practices in worship repertoire selection. Yet there are many excellent principles to consider:

- What melodies or texts feel like a part of the legacy of the place and have become a custom of the community? (For an excellent conversation about the significant difference between customs and traditions, I recommend Diana Butler Bass's book *The Practicing Congregation* [Rowman & Littlefield Publishers, 2004]). Can we ensure that some of those sacred moments of memory or ongoing familiarity are a part of our repertory?

- Are there certain thematics, texts, stories, or holidays that could be lifted up uniquely during a single gathering or over a short span of time that would require a wider repertoire beyond the familiar? These need not always be brand-new pieces but selections we share only when they are most appropriate. Where might they fit?

- If you and your partners would like to enhance a very specific moment in that day's or season's worship, which melodies or pieces would best bring that moment to life for the community? What melody would express that best, and how can we provide context? (Resist the impulse to pick a new piece because you just learned it and it's moving for worship. That may be true, but is it what this group needs at this time?)

- Can others in the community help me create success with those newer moments? Is there a chorus who can learn it in advance and help make it feel as if many in the community already know it, even if they're not leading but are singing in the pews? Do my co-clergy or co-leaders know the melody and can they be songleading partners in that moment?

As you map out the musical selections (as well as making space for poetry, responsive reading, silence, breath, movement, and listening), consider how the energy of the prayer will hold together. Are we asking for celebratory joy into immediate silent reflection with no transition between? Are we inviting people to stand and share sorrows and joys before we've built some communal trust and egalitarian connective singing?

Worship is its own work—and many of us, trained as clergy or spiritual leaders or without formal training, are asked to lead musical prayer or ritual moments. The questions outlined in this book all apply, and I would encourage you to gather more support systems and accountability thought partners as you craft your worship, and to tread sensitively when planning to lead prayer. Much of the consulting work I engage in is about creating prayerful worship that blends old and new, sung and spoken, in ways that are effective for communities.

School Setting

When we consider repertoire selection—the songs in our songleading tool kit—it will make a difference if you are asked to lead a one-off single session with young people or if you are hired to be an ongoing musical support for a group of students. For a single visit, you will want to know what repertoire the group already knows and what the organizers are hoping you will accomplish as a part of their larger pedagogic goal. At the same time, you likely won't want to teach a lot of new material that may not be reinforced by other songleaders or staff members after you depart. Sing something new and unique to you or that can be reinforced after you leave by the local leaders.

If you are going to be with a school or group of students for a longer period or a school year, you have the opportunity to build a curriculum and lay the groundwork for building a repertoire over time. In addition, by building an ongoing relationship with students, teachers, and staff, you can enhance the experiential nature of the singing experience. Beyond learning the songs, by singing together over time a group will grow in trust (with each other and with you), and you can begin to challenge them to sing in more complex forms like rounds, parts, and harmony, all with more confidence.

Knowing who the group is in their communal setting is crucial to selecting repertoire and style of singing.

Communal Setting

There is growing sensitivity in communal justice gatherings to the meaningful ways we can feature music that originated with cultures that may not be our own. Many partners and organizations can help you think about how to explain a piece of music's roots or sacred story. Planning for such events should include a wide range of voices as a natural part of the process. A case in point:

In the United States, each year around the weekend commemorating the life of revered civil rights leader Dr. Martin Luther King, Jr., opportunities arise to share music and memory that connects the Jewish American and African American experiences. Both Jews and non-Jews of color are often absent from the conversation around repertoire and how we tell our stories in ways that give voice to these shared experiences while honoring those unique narratives. After years of singing melodies that come from the lived experiences of enslaved peoples in this country superimposed with Hebrew lyrics from the texts that voice the Jewish struggle for freedom, I have become more thoughtful in how I select and lead this repertoire.

Guided by Jews of color who share the experiences of both communities, as well as in conversation with accountability partners of color in communal-singing spaces, I am much more intentional about how I share the roots and history of a given melody. While our experiences are not the same, we can tell parallel stories that in the echoes between them honor the history and struggle for freedom of a variety of people while offering a way for others to access and empathize with that struggle.

Just as I began this book writing about the accessibility of all bodies in space and the necessary awareness of everyone's uniqueness, I want to emphasize here again the key principle "Not about us without us." Just as many of us choose to live in a world that values equity, justice, and inclusion, our songleading work must be built on the relationships necessary to understand the roots of our repertoire, as well as how we can share melodies that come from a variety of sources with sensitivity, transparency, and an authentic desire to include everyone in the conversation.

While there are many who are writing and teaching about how we share repertoire from other cultures in sensitive ways, I have learned that taking the time to engage with partners with whom you may be sharing the program (or reaching out to accountability partners who may not be in the room but who can help you explain a piece of music's roots or sacred story) will help the community feel safe in the experience.

ॐ

Knowing the makeup of the group can help you not only select an appropriate song, but prepare to share it or sing it together with sensitivity.

For more information on repertoire, please see appendix H, "Songleading Resources," page 124. For more information on memorizing and learning songs, see appendix A, "How to Memorize a Song," page 113 and appendix B, "How to Learn a Song," page 114.

·10·

Conclusion

IN WRITING THIS BOOK, I reviewed my thesis submitted for my masters in sacred music from Hebrew Union College–Jewish Institute of Religion, titled "Cantors and Campers: Bringing Youth into the Worship Service." I was pleased to find that while my core philosophy remains consistent, I have developed a much more expansive understanding of how songleading can transform a shared space, whether that's a synagogue or a classroom, a convention or a rally.

"Communal music substantiates a community with low hierarchic expectations by confirming the equality of the group," I declared in 2001. "The power of the music lies less in its own compositional merit than it does in its function as community builder."

If the songs are architecture, you, the songleader, are the architect who curates the elements and carefully arranges them so there may be a sacred house in which your group will dwell.

I want to emphasize something as we near the end: songleading is not an exact science; nor is it easy. There are so many variables for the leader, including lyrics, melody, instrumentation, communication, and body language. And there are unlimited variables for the group: their having a different knowledge base than you anticipated, bad weather changing a room, their energy being too low or their energy too high. A lot can go wrong despite the most thorough preparation.

A skilled songleader should be able to pivot and make changes before or sometimes even during the leading of a song. There is a natural improvisational element to songleading—it requires flexibility, the comfort to be nimble and make changes, and a freedom to know that the outcome is not altogether clear or in your control.

It is okay to make mistakes. If you forget the lyrics, ask the group for help. If you planned a key that is now too high or you just forgot what key you planned and you realize too late that you're in the wrong key, just call out, "Let's drop an octave—it's too high!" Sometimes you may find you don't remember a piece as well as you thought you did, and you don't have the sheet music in front of you. It happens to all of us.

As much as you prepare, sometimes things just don't work. You try again the next time. As my teacher, friend, and songleading colleague Cantor Ellen Dreskin says, "Failure is only failure if you don't learn anything from it."

Hopefully, you found new learning in these pages. Be solid in your why, be confident in your skills, have your ears open, and carry a diverse and nimble repertoire. In doing so, you will be ready to be of service.

ONE LAST STORY

At the end of a Hava Nashira weekend—the annual conference for songleaders, educators, and worship leaders at Camp OSRUI in Ocono-mowoc, Wisconsin—I turned to my colleague and asked, "So, were we successful?" She replied, "We planned for who we thought our partic-ipants were. We led with humility and humor. We made *many* mistakes, but we listened, we watched, and we sang. Our people came with dif-ferent needs, and they left connected more deeply with themselves, each other, and their world."

I'd call that success.

·Appendix A·
How to Memorize a Song

Start with the **chorus** or **most repetitive part** of the song:

• Memorize words by repeating them quickly to yourself in rhythm. If you are not using a guitar, this may be the main step. If you know the melody well but are only learning the lyric, say the words to yourself repeatedly. Memorize the first word of each line and that may help you remember the words that follow.

• If you plan to play guitar, play through the chords once or twice with the lyrics and sing along. Make sure you are memorizing the chords in the key in which you plan to lead the song.

• If there are multiple lines, start with one line or two lines at a time.

• Play the chords quickly, over and over again. Don't spend time singing it in full voice.

• Run through the chords in your head without the guitar as you walk around.

• Identify patterns—e.g., in this chorus a G chord always follows a D. You don't need to look at the chord sheet; just remember that.

• Think of a trick or mnemonic to memorize the chords.

• If you have music theory background, you may memorize chords by their scale degree (I, IV, V, etc.).

For **verses** or a **bridge**, the steps are the same. However, you may need to spend a bit more time on the chords if they are not as repetitive.

As you memorize, pay attention to chord patterns that are repetitive. Make sure that you're *listening* while you're memorizing; over time, certain melodic phrases will guide you to the next chord, or you'll find that your educated guess is close to correct.

If you do not have chord sheets and are learning a song by ear, figuring out the chords also helps you to memorize them.

·Appendix B·
How to Learn a Song
by Cantor Jeff Klepper

1. Add it to your song catalog as a "Song to Learn." Note where and when you first heard it.
2. Record, copy, or download it. (Or have someone who knows it sing it for you.)
3. Add the recording to a device you keep with you, so you can play it anywhere. (While you're at it, dream it and soak it up.)
4. Check the internet for lyrics and/or chords, or figure them out for yourself.
5. Print out a lyric sheet with the chords. Try different keys to find the best one for you.
6. Go over the words, and check the source.
7. If the lyrics are in a foreign language, check the source, text, pronunciation, and translation.
8. Try to find a published notated version and check it against your version.
9. Notate the song yourself, by hand, on music paper. Sight-read the notes on "la," or play them on any instrument you can play.
10. Keep a notebook or folder with all the songs you are working on.
11. Practice the chords while humming, until you memorize them.
12. Try to pick out the melody by ear (in a simple key) on guitar or piano.
13. Work out any problems that arise with melody, words, or chords.
14. Break the song into sections (verse, chorus, bridge, or A, B, C).
15. Try singing the song with different rhythms and tempi.
16. Sing the song over and over. Sing it in the car (if socially acceptable).
17. Sing the song with friends or family. Create your own harmo-

nies.

18. Before you teach it, practice stopping and starting each phrase.
19. Teach or sing the song to anyone who will sit for five minutes and listen.
20. Imagine singing the song in different contexts, moods, and situations.

[Used by permission of Jeff Klepper.]

·Appendix C·
How to Teach a Song

PREPARATION

Words:
1. Learn the pronunciation.
2. Look up the translation (if applicable).
3. Source: Where does the text come from?
4. Message: Why this song? What do you want it to convey?

Music:
1. Know the composer.
2. Find a good key.
3. Learn the melody backward and forward.

Extras:
1. Find the right breaks, and practice the teach line-by-line.
2. If there are good harmonies, when might you introduce them?
3. If the song is a round, when might you separate the group? Do you need support to lead the parts of the round?

BREAKING DOWN THE TEACH

1. Intro: Say something about the song and why it matters.
2. Sing through the whole song or
   Sing through the grabber/hook/chorus.
       - Review the words (optional).
3. Break up the chorus.
       - Sing a line, two lines, or part of a line, and invite all
         to sing back to you.
4. Sing the whole chorus together.
5. Sing through the verse.
       - Review the words (optional).
6. Break up the verse as you did the chorus in number 3.

7. Sing the verse all together.
8. Sing the chorus and verse altogether.
9. Add extra parts (harmonies, hand motions, claps, etc.).

Making mistakes (big and little) is okay.

Don't be afraid to stop and get the pronunciation or melody just right—teaching new music is mostly about *listening!*

·*Appendix D*·
Know Your People

WORSHIP SETTING

- What does it mean to pray in this community?
- Is there an area of liturgy or prayer in general that the leadership would like the community to be focused on?
- What are the "sacred cows," the elements of your worship that are crucial to create safety, familiarity, and trust?
- Will you have the opportunity to be in relationship with the community before you lead them in prayer?
- What does the space look like, and is there any flexibility?
- When all is said and done, what would you like the participants to say that they experienced as they leave your time together?
- In conversations with professional and lay leaders, ask about the makeup of the community and who they expect to attend the worship. Has there been a loss to recognize or a joyous event to celebrate?
- Where are you in the life cycle of the community, the calendar of their religious tradition? Where are you in the life cycle of that institution or community—for example, the installation of new leadership, dedication of a building, or formation of a new student group?
- Do people travel great distances to join in fellowship, or is it a local/walking community? Do people attend as a family? Are there usually children? If so, of what age(s), and what is the expectation about decorum, noise, and youth involvement?
- What is the vision and mission of the congregation, and how is that manifest in the worship and musical choices of the community? Does the community lean into social justice and use prayer as a way to galvanize the commitment to sacred work in the world? Or do they value moments of silence, introspection, solitude, and meditation?

- Will the people know each other and value relationship building within the worship, or is the goal more toward being moved and led by leaders "at the front"?

SCHOOL SETTING

- Will there be other staff support in the program with you? What is their expectation about their role (are they on "off-hour" coffee break, or do they help as leading partners and engaging with students)?
- Where will the children be coming from as they begin singing time, and where are they going when your session is finished?
- Is there any educational content, learning, holiday, or value the teachers are working on that you can help to reinforce or use music to enhance?

COMMUNITY SETTING

- Are groups from different communities, clubs, or faiths gathering, or is it a fairly homogoneous group?
- Who are the other presentors, speakers, or musicians who might be sharing content? Is there a chance to partner with them and learn more about what they will be offering?
- What do the people who are gathering expect to happen? Why are they there?
- Who is the person in charge who can help you make changes on site?

·*Appendix E*·
Know Your Space

WORSHIP SETTING

- When might it be helpful to be on a raised platform and when might you want to stand on the floor, closer to the participants? Will you have sound that is portable in both locations? Will people in the back be able to see and hear you clearly?

- Are people looking down into text, a book, or a handout? Do you need to get their attention to indicate any musical moments with your body, instrument, or facial cues? Are people looking at screens above you, behind you, or next to you? Where is the best place to stand—should the focus be on the screen or you, or are there opportunities for both?

- Is the worship music designed to create communal singing, or are there moments for reflection and meditation? What space usage might help you achieve each of those styles of engagement?

- Are there partner participants, and where are they located? Are there co-clergy or co-leaders? Is there a choir or band, and are they intended to be the focus? Is the congregational voice the focus? To where are people's eyes drawn, and are you aware of and in control of that choice?

SCHOOL SETTING

- Will the students be at round tables, so some will have their back to you and may grumble when asked to turn around?

- Will they all be seated on the ground? If so, will you have a chair to sit on? Must you stand, creating distance from your group?

- Are you placed in front of a window where the students will be distracted by other kids on a playground?

- Can you sit on the floor near the children?

- Are you asking them to move a lot, but they are seated at chair/desk combinations or round tables that are positioned very close

together?
- Can the children have full freedom of movement in their space? Will they be in a large space where they can easily move farther away from you and your control?
- Will you need to be able to have access to each student, to get close, to tap someone, or to pass out an object?

COMMUNITY SETTING
- How many people will be sitting or standing, and for how long?
- Is the room too big for the number of people gathered? Can you make it more intimate?
- Is everyone wound up and excited, and ready to march? Will there be lots of talking and a general lack of focus?
- Are there placards, signs, or banners causing sight-line disruption?
- Is there mediocre or no sound support?
- Are you prepared for last-minute additions, cancellations, and changes to timing?

QUESTIONS TO CONSIDER WHEN EVALUATING A SPACE
- Where will you be placed?
- Are you higher than the participants or on the same plane?
- Is the seating fixed or flexible? If it's flexible, do you have permission and support to move the seats?
- Are participants seated at tables or in rows? Are people standing?
- Will there be visuals like a screen or a board that will require a sight line?
- Is the room a smaller space than would comfortably accommodate the numbers of expected participants, or is it larger?
- Are there windows? Where are they in relation to you and the group?
- Is there a sound system and vocal projection support?
- Is there easy mobility and accessibility in the singing space?
- Can people move around if you want them to or if you don't want them to?

·*Appendix F*·
Setting Goals

Goal setting for any singing moment is crucial. Here are some questions to help you refine your goal:

- Why are we gathered at this moment?
- What or how should we feel (about ourselves, our faith, or the world) when we finish singing together?
- What have I been asked to do? Do I have a clear set of outcomes and measures of success, or did I begin goal setting with too little information?
- How would I like the group to feel and what would I like them to know or understand when we finish singing together?
- What are the traps I often fall into as a songleader? (For example, do I worry too much about my voice? Do I get overly nervous about my guitar skills? Do I not ask enough of the group?)
- What does the group need from me? How can I learn more about the people I will be singing with? Do I ask leaders and participants about their gathering or experiences? Is there an opportunity to spend time with the group before I will be singing (a meal, a program previous, or another session)?

As always, being in the moment, you want to find the joyous intersection of planning and spontaneity, where you are both well-prepared as well as listening intently and being fully in the moment.

·*Appendix G*·
Songleading Outdoors

When singing or playing outdoors, sound has nowhere to bounce as it does indoors—it goes right up into the wide-open space. This is also true for the group's voices, so if you want to hear beautiful singing from the group, that is hard to achieve outdoors. Here are some important considerations when songleading in the great wide open:

- Sound amplification will be crucial. Keep in mind that when the wind blows, it will make distracting noises into your microphone.
- Unless you're in a very controlled location outside, it's easy for people to sit far apart, roam, and create distance in numerous ways. Consider how you can "block" people into a close area near you.
- Things like grass, bugs, hot sun, and dirt can be distractions.
- Will people be expected to sit on the grass? Is someone bringing out chairs and intending to return them?
- Where is the rain location should the weather become inclement?
- If you need materials like lyrics for yourself, where will they be? If you plan to use a music stand, bring clothesline or binder clips to attach your pages to the stand—they will blow away without them; I guarantee it!
- If the group needs lyrics, will they get paper handouts, assuming there is no outdoor screen capability? If you have screens outdoors, consider the time of day, location of the sun, and the ability to see screens in broad daylight.
- If it's very sunny, you might find it more comfortable to wear sunglasses. I strongly encourage you not to do so. While it's uncomfortable to squint, wearing sunglasses while you songlead cuts off the community's connection to you and makes it nearly impossible to sing along, particularly in an already challenging environment.

·*Appendix H*·
Songleading Resources

- Attend music and songleading conferences. Networking with folks sharing the same pursuit can be just the thing you need.
- Search for repertoire online, but be careful to check sources. Make sure you translate texts before you use them.
- Find an accountability partner—someone with whom you can road test your choices. Additional partners could be found from clergy or experts in languages that aren't vernacular.
- Be an aggressive listener of music; mine the resources of music collections and archives.
- Be an interpreter of what you hear and love into both your own voice and what your group needs to take from it. Adapt it for the people's or situation's needs.
- Make use of books containing songleading standards, including *Rise Up Singing* (Sing Out!, 1988) and *The Complete Shireinu* (Transcontinental Music Publications, 2001).

BOOKS MADE REFERENCE TO IN *SONGLEADING: A WORK OF ART*

Merri Lovinger Arian. *Leveling the Praying Field: Methods and Melodies to Elevate Congregational Worship.* Transcontinental Music Publications, 2018.

Diana Butler Bass. *The Practicing Congregation: Imagining a New Old Church.* Rowman & Littlefield Publishers, 2004.

Alice Parker. *The Gift of Song.* GIA Publications, 2020.

Joey Weisenberg. *Building Singing Communities: A Practical Guide to Unlocking the Power of Music in Jewish Prayer.* Hadar, 2011.

Cantor Rosalie Will
brings more than twenty-five years of experience in training songleaders, leading worship, and creating singing communities. After sixteen years as cantor of Temple Emanuel in Kensington, Maryland, she now consults congregations on issues of worship, music, and synagogue transition, visits congregations for Shabbat and weekend residencies to further explore new ideas of worship and prayer, and mentors clergy in the field. She is founder and executive  director of Sing Unto God, a new nonprofit dedicated to elevating the practice and promotion of meaningful worship and of singing together. She produces events that lead the cutting-edge of worship and music thinking and trains professionals on best principles for communal singing, as well as singing for justice. Rosalie also supports the Union for Reform Judaism on issues of worship and music as a consultant.

Rosalie was ordained by the Debbie Friedman School of Sacred Music of Hebrew Union College–Jewish Institute of Religion in New York and served as vice president for member relations of the American Conference of Cantors. She is a proud product of URJ camps and NFTY, received her undergraduate degree in Jewish studies from the University of Pennsylvania, and lives in a Maryland suburb of Washington, DC, with her daughters and her partner.

You can find more information about Cantor Rosalie Will at rosaliewill.com and about Sing Unto God at singuntogod.org.